W9-BOL-984

CROQUET

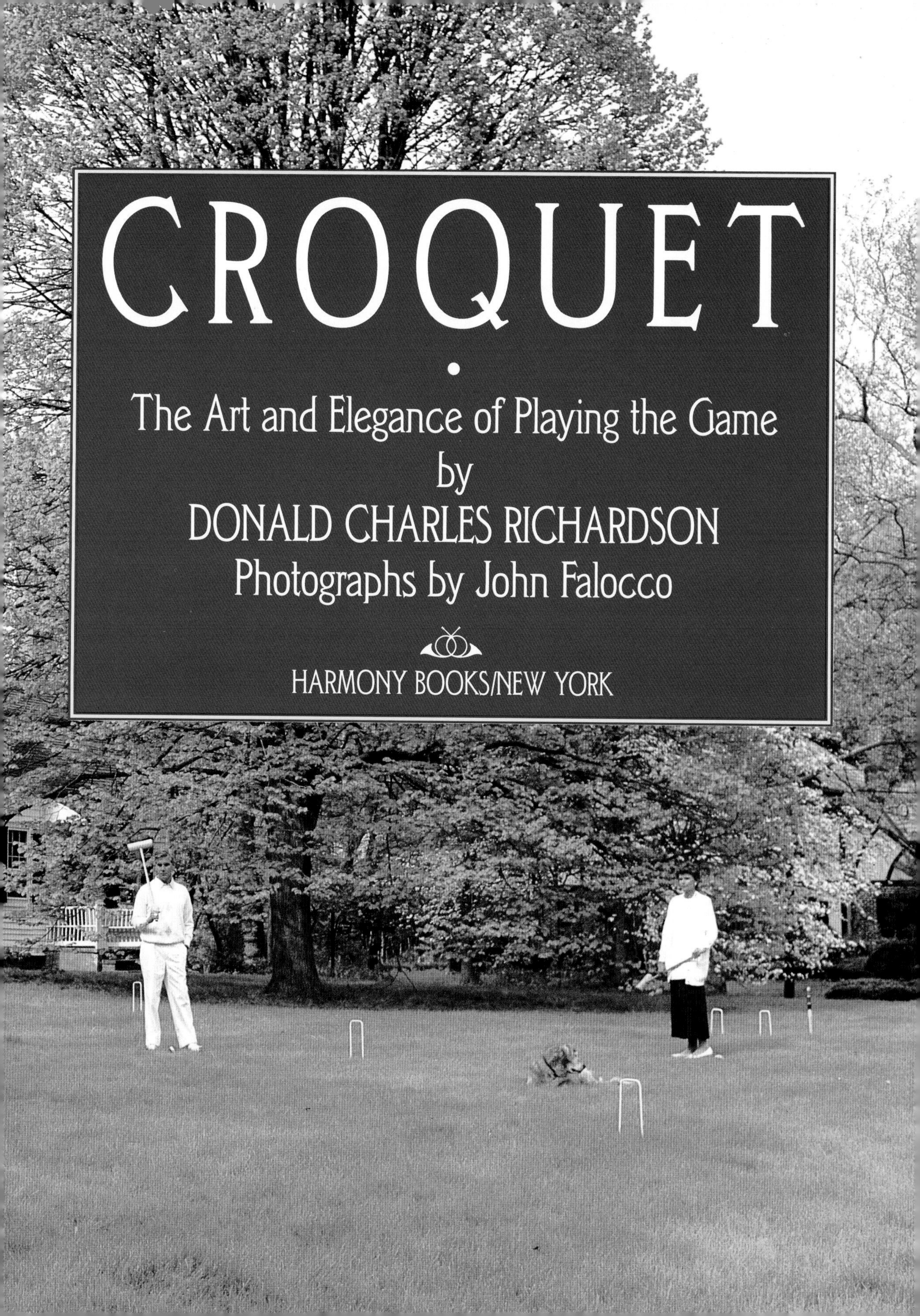

CROQUET

·

The Art and Elegance of Playing the Game
by
DONALD CHARLES RICHARDSON
Photographs by John Falocco

HARMONY BOOKS/NEW YORK

Design: Ken Sansone
Game's Master: Lawrence J. Gazlay
Stylist: Gabriela Hirsch
Hair and Makeup: Michael D'Apice,
Vinnie Ferrara, Kathleen Murphy, and Glen Solberg

Copyright © 1988 by Donald Charles Richardson

All rights reserved. No part of this book may be reproduced
or transmitted in any form or by any means, electronic or
mechanical, including photocopying, recording,
or by any information storage and retrieval system,
without permission in writing from the publisher.

Published by Harmony Books, a division of Crown Publishers, Inc.,
225 Park Avenue South, New York, New York 10003
and represented in Canada by the Canadian MANDA Group

HARMONY and colophon are trademarks of Crown Publishers, Inc.

Manufactured in Japan

LIBRARY OF CONGRESS CATALOGING-IN-PUBLICATION DATA
Richardson, Donald Charles.
Croquet: the art and elegance of playing the game.
Includes index.
1. Croquet.   I. Title.
GV931.R43   1988   796.35′4   87-25200

ISBN 0-517-56826-7
10 9 8 7 6 5 4 3 2 1
First Edition

TO ANN, JOEL, AND LARRY—FOR
ALL THE LOVE AND LAUGHTER

●

CONTENTS

CROQUET

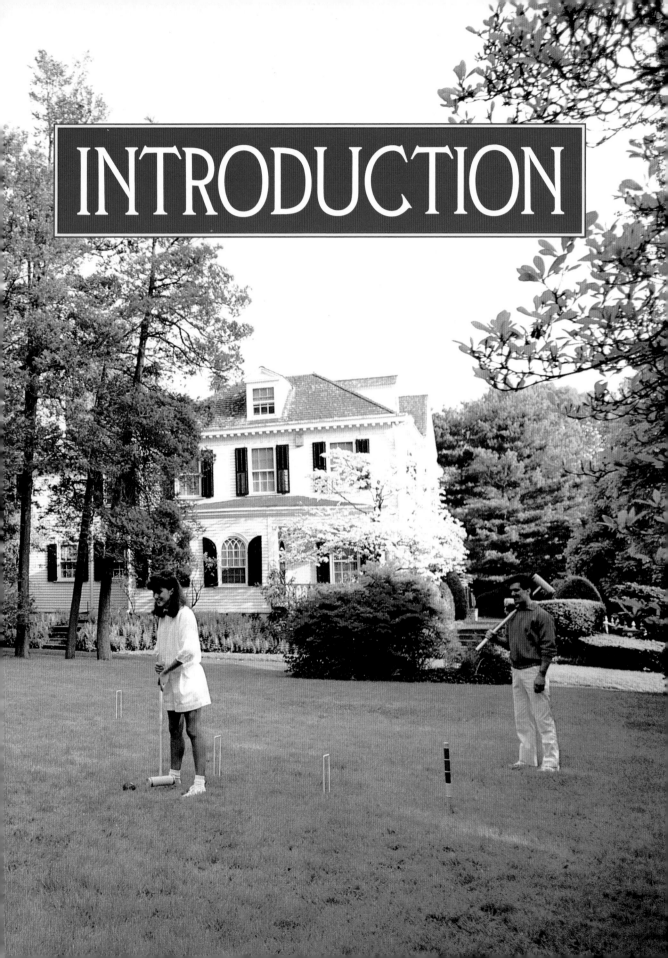

INTRODUCTION

roquet has always been considered one of the most elegant and civilized of games. And its current popularity in backyards across North America can be easily explained. Croquet is charming, fun, competitive, and provides an organized afternoon's entertainment for families and friends.

The lure of this very special pastime is also enhanced by the wonderful auras of romance and nostalgia that embrace it. Just a mention of or passing reference to croquet is usually enough to evoke, for many people, a wonderful series of images and memories: warm, sunny days punctuated by the voices of friendly gatherings, or late afternoons when the only sounds breaking the summer stillness are quiet taps as mallets and balls make contact and gentle sighs of resignation as

shadows lengthen across green lawns, bringing the activity to a hurried close.

The game of croquet has traditionally been surrounded by an atmosphere of quiet graciousness. And still today it is not possible to pick up a mallet and set out to play without feeling at least a little of the mystique created when our Victorian ancestors made their stately entrances onto the court and began their competitions.

Since its introduction into polite society, croquet, like most other games, has been subject to enthusiasms and fashionable trends, alternately reaching the peaks of popularity and then slipping into periods of decline. But it has never fallen fully into obscurity. Somewhere, there has always been someone with a set of equipment and a lively interest in the game. Through the years, croquet has tenaciously remained a part of American and English sporting history (every June, tennis fans are reminded that the name of the site where the most famous matches are held is the All-England Lawn Tennis and Croquet Club) and has maintained continuous social acceptance never equaled by any other backyard activity.

Despite traditional misconceptions, the game of croquet is not limited to North American or English lawns. It was naturally exported to the far reaches of the British Empire and is still played in Bermuda, South Africa, Australia, New Zealand, Canada, and Scotland. And recently, croquet has made its appearance in some rather unusual and far-flung places.

For example, retired Communist officials in the People's Republic of China have developed a fascination for the game and play it constantly on, of all things, clay basketball courts rather than the traditional grass lawns. These games, incidentally, are not casual affairs where guests drop by and are offered mallets, but dignified events to which participants must be formally invited.

Although croquet was played in the Soviet Union at the American embassy by Ambassador Averell Harriman (who, it is rumored, refused to accept the post unless a croquet court was installed on the embassy lawn), it was not until recently that the Russian upper

Taking Croquet. Wood engraving.
Courtesy of John Jaques Co.

OPPOSITE: *Placing the Ball for a Croquet.*
Wood engraving from *How to Play Croquet*
(Boston, Amsden and Co., 1865).

classes began playing on private courts. An interesting sidelight to Soviet attraction to croquet is their scientific investigations into the game. Soviet technicians have concluded that playing croquet is an excellent pastime for their cosmonauts, offering a calming and relaxing effect on both the minds and bodies of the men and women who travel through space and must readjust to earthly conditions.

The appreciation of croquet around the world, as well as its position as the mainstay of backyard games in America, is due to the fact that it's a perfect pastime for so many people. It is a game for everyone. Croquet has no requirements that limit it to any particular sex or age group. Both men and women, as well as children, can become excellent players. When a family or group of friends wants to be outdoors, involved in an activity, and is not inclined to great exertion, croquet is the ideal endeavor. This fascinating game allows for conversation and socializing, accompanied by the challenge of skillful competition.

And it is, or will most probably become for many people, truly a competition. Since croquet can be played with varying degrees of expertise from a series of casual and simple strokes to intricate strategies and complex maneuvers, it is important to realize that there is a definite difference between croquet the *sport* and croquet the *game*. Both are intriguing, and the level of play for either is basically dependent on the talents and efforts players are willing to invest.

Croquet the sport employs only six wickets and is played on very carefully laid-out courts by master players who have often invested a considerable amount of money in their equipment, have trained rigidly for competition, and view croquet as a tense and concentrated

ABOVE: **Wood engraving depicting croquet.**
OPPOSITE: *Croquet*, Gustave Doré.

form of intelligent combat. The mallets for the sport are large and heavy, and the wickets narrow, only slightly wider than the croquet balls, thus making entrance and exit difficult. Also, there is only one stake in tournament croquet, and most important, the rules are markedly different and more demanding than those used for the backyard game. The sport of croquet is played throughout the United States, with the center for competition in Florida, where the headquarters of the United States Croquet Association is located.

The requirements for the game of croquet are considerably less complicated. And although the game can reach the same level of cutthroat competition and expertise as the sport, backyard croquet is usually a more casual activity, meant to be relaxing and fun. It is played on a grass lawn of almost any size with nine wickets and a variety of mallet sizes (depending on the manufacturer). Backyard croquet can be enjoyed for an investment of as little as twenty dollars.

Croquet is about the game. It includes the history of croquet, the rules for backyard play, standardized by the United States Croquet Association, a discussion of the types and quality of equipment available, along with instructions on how to lay out a croquet court, grip the mallet, and achieve versatile, useful, and even dramatic strokes. There is a chapter on entertaining which includes recipes for a croquet picnic, luncheon, and tea, and anecdotes about familiar people who have played in the past. Also, golf croquet, a variation of the basic croquet game, is included with its rules, court layout, and description.

Croquet is designed to lure you from your porch, patio, or deck into the backyard. In these pages, you will find all you need to know about enjoying and playing the game and creating a gracious afternoon's entertainment for yourself and your friends.

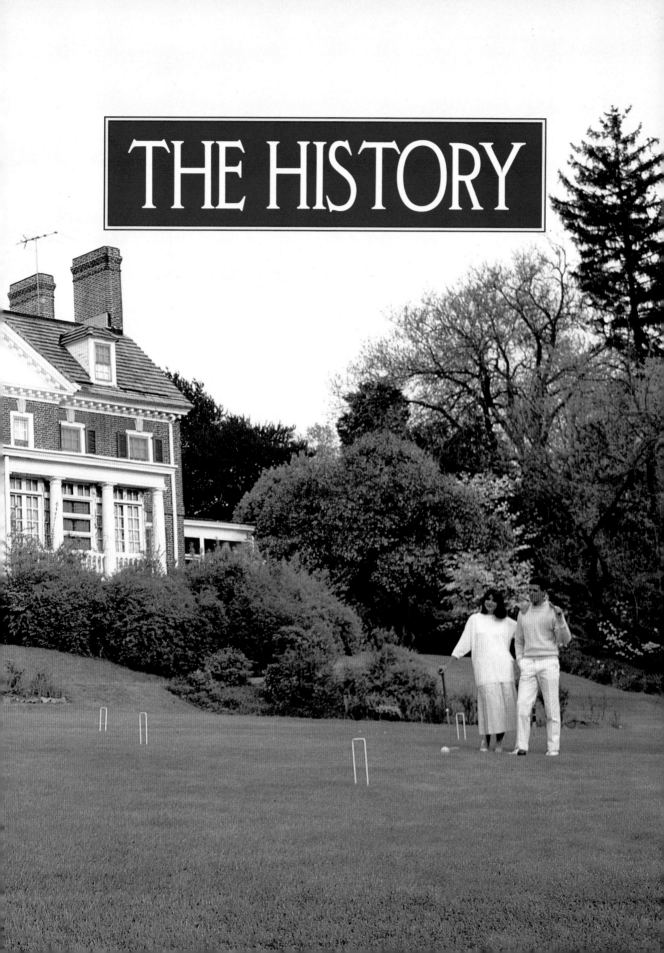

THE HISTORY

The word *croquet* comes from the French word *crochet,* which means "crooked stick." And according to R.C.A. Prior, M.D., F.L.S., author of the 1872 treatise *Notes on Croquet and Some Ancient Bat and Ball Games Relating to It,* "Who invented croquet, or who improved a rustic game into one fit for polite society, is a question that has often been asked and has never been answered." Despite the fact that Dr. Prior utilizes the French, English, Greek, Latin, and German languages in his supremely elegant text, he doesn't answer the question either.

Regardless of croquet's authentic origins, it is accepted that our game is an adaptation of the game *pallemaille,* played in France during the fourteenth century. Croquet traveled from France to England, via Ireland, during the reign of Charles II and was played in an area named for the game. The street in London that still bears the anglicized name, Pall Mall, was originally a croquet court.

After a brief period of popularity, croquet went out of style until around 1850 when John Jaques, a toymaker in London, created a complete set of equipment and reintroduced the game to fashionable society. This innovative action resulted in an incredible enthusiasm for croquet. In fact, the English became so passionately devoted to the game that special wickets bearing candles were set up so that play could continue well into the night. Croquet was the game of polite society until about 1870 when lawn tennis became the rage and the popularity of croquet slipped from its exalted position.

At about this same time, croquet was introduced into the United States to resounding success. Americans, including President Rutherford B. Hayes, became enthralled with the game and were soon avid players. Although not well remembered for an inspiring administration, President Hayes *did* allocate six dollars from the government treasury to buy "good quality" croquet balls. This profligate spending was vociferously condemned by his Democratic opponents in Congress. Croquet became so popular Americans employed their ingenuity to finding a way of playing indoors.

Parlor croquet must have been a somewhat peculiar pastime in formal American drawing rooms. There were two versions. The first, set out across the floor, was called carpet croquet and used carpet tacks to hold up the wickets. (Just what condition the room was left in is unknown.)

Board croquet utilized a five-foot-by-three-foot board covered with baize, which was placed on a table. The balls were one inch in diameter and made of either glass or ivory, and the mallets had handles eight inches long. The basic rules were essentially the same as for the outdoor contest, except that any player who drove his opponent's ball off the

ABOVE: **John Jaques II.**

OPPOSITE: **Two 1869 wood engravings by Winslow Homer. Bowdoin College Museum of Art.**

"Unlike most out-of-door sports, it does not require the possession of great strength or powers of endurance, or severe muscular exertion on the part of the player. Excellence in it is almost equally attainable to the weakly and delicate as to the healthy and robust. Old and young meet on its arena on more nearly equal terms than in any other known game or skill. A 'correct eye,' steady heads and nerves, and good judgement are the essential qualifications for a good croquet player, and the possession of these advantages, of course, is not dependent upon the age, sex, or condition of the person."

From *Croquet: Its Principles and Rules*
by A. Rover
Milton Bradley and Co., 1871

board (and onto the floor) had to start over again. It is interesting and somehow charming to imagine several elegant ladies opulently gowned searching under massive furniture for a tiny, wayward croquet ball.

But of course the most important arena was the lawn. Many of the new social elite had enormous country houses with extensive grounds, ideal for setting up a croquet court. And it was soon considered very stylish to invite guests to participate in the new, very popular, and highly "moral" (a quality considered very important) game.

But unfortunately the assured and much-lauded morality of croquet was soon to prove somewhat tenuous. It was discovered that young people in particular found croquet an enjoyable pastime because it gave them a chance to be with members of the opposite

Palo Alto Spring, Thomas Hill. Oil on canvas, 1878. Stanford University Museum of Art.

ABOVE: *The Croquet Players*,
Winslow Homer. Chalk on paper.
The Metropolitan Museum of Art.

OPPOSITE, ABOVE: *Croquet.*
From *Cassall's Household Guide*, 1875.

OPPOSITE, BELOW LEFT: *Croquet.*
Sheet music cover, c. 1850.

OPPOSITE, BELOW RIGHT: The enthusiasm for
croquet began in the summer of 1866.

OVERLEAF: *Croquet Players*, Winslow Homer.
Oil on canvas, 1865. Albright-Knox
Gallery, Buffalo, New York.

sex without the restrictive influence of their chaperons. (Victorian rule books attempted to control this potentially dangerous situation by stressing the importance of players not taking too much time between their shots. This rule was not only intended to keep the game going but was also designed to limit the amount of time available for flirtation between the young innocents.)

In addition, there were also occasions during play when a lady's ankle might be exposed to the wandering eyes of the men (keen eyesight has always been an advantage in croquet). Conservative society also rather belatedly realized that croquet was an activity in which men and women could meet on an equal footing. Men traditionally had their exclusively male outdoor sports, which women were occasionally allowed to watch. However, croquet not only offered the ladies a chance to participate in a game but gave them the

"As to its introduction into this country [England] the meager result of all the inquiries that I have been able to make is only this: that I learned from Mr Spratt, of 18 Brook Street, Hanover Square, that more than twenty years ago a Miss Macnaghten brought it to him as a game that had been lately introduced into Ireland, but which she had first seen on the continent in its primitive state—in the South of France, or in Italy, for he forgets which she said—and described as of the simplest and most rustic in character. . . . Mr Spratt has still in his possession her letter in which she had drawn up the rules as observed by the peasantry of that country, and will show it to anyone who is curious upon the subject. This poor lady was accidentally burnt to death, and probably we shall never get any more information on the subject. Mr Spratt kept the implements in his shop for some years, and finding no demand for them, sold the game to Mr Jaques, an enterprising young man who brought it into notice, and no doubt has realized a fortune by it, as he certainly deserved to do."

From *Notes on Croquet and Some Ancient Bat and Ball Games Related to It,* 1872 by R.C.A. Prior, M.D., F.L.S.

Preparing to Take Croquet.
Wood engraving, 1865.

opportunity to play *against the men*. They were, in effect, challenging the superiority of the males . . . and often winning! Bah. An unheard-of idea.

There were other, somewhat symbolic sensations that rigid parents weren't sure they understood but were positive they disliked. When a female player was able to hit a male player's croquet ball and then croquet it, the placing of her foot on his croquet ball equaled emasculation. And, suggestively, the actual progress around the court could be viewed as a form of sexual pursuit. The possibly inferred prize at the end of the contest was a matter of deep, very shocking, and thoroughly satisfying thought for the older ladies.

If these problems weren't enough, when it was discovered that some young men were laying bets on the outcome of the contest, croquet was in deep trouble. Suddenly the game gained a reputation for being dangerous and fast. The word *croquet* itself actually became a euphemism for flirtation, and the slang created by the game ("sent up Salt River," for example, was a term used when a ball suffered croquet) was even being employed in the drawing room. This whole situation was obviously unacceptable.

In the late 1890s, the city of Boston banned croquet. The tremors of this stunningly preposterous act created distress about the game across the country. Self-righteous ministers shouted from their pulpits about the decadence of croquet, and one religious magazine, full of misplaced zeal and

"The excitement towards the end of the game often becomes intense, and each stroke is watched with the keenest interest. Gradually, one-by-one, the players hit the post, until perhaps only two remain, and now occurs an opportunity for skillful play. The object of both is to hit the post, and failing in that, to keep as far off his adversary as he can. Each endeavors, at the same time drawing nearer to the great object in view, to keep the post between his and the other ball. At length one plays at the post, misses it, and sends his ball near his adversary, who first hits it, next croquets it away, and then strikes the post, and wins the victory."

From *Croquet: Its Principles and Rules* by A. Rover Milton Bradley and Co., 1871

indignation, condemned croquet as "the gaping jaws of Hades." While we view this behavior as overreactionary and laughable today, the hellfire-and-damnation attitude of the nouveau riche was powerful enough to effec-

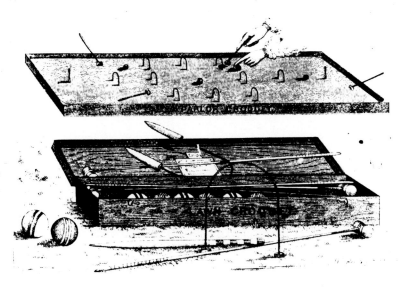

A croqueterie held equipment for both lawn and parlor games. Wood engraving from *Croquet, Its Principles and Rules,* Milton Bradley and Co., 1867.

"Once he had spent a week-end in a country house the King liked to be given the same bedroom, sitting-room, dressing-room and bathroom on each succeeding visit; and he liked to follow the same sort of daily routine. If he were not going out shooting, he would have breakfast in his room and then attend to any correspondence there might be, his letters being opened for him by a servant who stood behind his chair and slit the envelopes with a long paper-knife. Towards midday he would go down to join the other guests and perhaps go for a stroll in the garden, making comments on any alterations his sharp eye noticed as having taken place since his last visit, or play a game of croquet which he and his partner usually won as everyone knew how cross he got if he was beaten. When staying with Sir Ernest Cassel he was often pitted against the Duchess of Sermoneta, who was not only extremely pretty but also a very bad player so that a game with her always put him in a good mood. One day, however, a lucky hit sent her ball flying 'right across the ground,' she recorded in her memoirs, 'and straight through the right hoop (I didn't even know it was the right one) and, continuing its glorious career, hit the King's ball straight into the rose bushes. . . . By the icy stillness that prevailed I realized that never, never was such a thing to happen again.'"

From *The Royal Victorians: King Edward VII, His Family and Friends*
by Christopher Hibbert

tively diminish America's enthusiasm for croquet for some time.

In the following years the popularity of croquet bounced back and forth between England and America, each country taking turns being fascinated with and then disinterested in the game. For instance, at the time of croquet's demise (on moral grounds) in the United States, there was another rebirth of the game in Britain during the period of Edwardian grandeur. Amid this opulent time, great country houses with large and lush lawns were very fashionable. The king loved croquet so much he took his set to Baden-Baden when he went for his annual cure. And when he visited country houses, croquet was considered a perfect game for entertaining dignified society. Croquet clubs were formed, and eventually there were more than 150 of these organizations in Great Britain.

English interest in croquet continued until World War I created other priorities. It is interesting to note that at one point croquet was considered so important, it was included in the 1904 Olympic Games. The only winner of a gold medal in croquet was an American, Charles Jacob from Springfield, Connecticut.

At the end of the war croquet resurfaced, but unfortunately in England it was discovered that several of the croquet clubs had lost so many members to the conflict that they were no longer operational.

In the United States, croquet took a peculiar twist. America had relented of most of its moral outrage after the turn of the century, and the game had been casually played throughout the country since that time. But a new center of croquet enthusiasm was established in the 1920s when it became popular

OPPOSITE: *Croquet*, **Will Barnet.**
Courtesy of Kennedy Galleries, Inc., New York.

with, of all people, the members of the Algonquin Round Table, a group of literary-minded individuals who met daily for lunch at the famous hotel, led by the redoubtable Alexander Woollcott. The portly theater critic took to the court at his and others' country houses against fellow literary lights such as Herbert Bayard Swope, Dorothy Parker, George Kaufman, and Moss Hart. At times they were joined by Harpo Marx and Richard Rodgers. Like several of the players, these games could be acrimonious in the extreme, with hostilities spilling over into dinners and even at times causing some of the participants to cease speaking to one another.

These people were devoted to croquet. So much so that once during a game at the estate of the same Ambassador Harriman who insisted on having croquet in the Soviet Union, eight men with snow plows and shovels were hired to clean the court during a stormy Thanksgiving contest.

> *"Talbott's estate was particularly prized for its glass-smooth croquet court. One evening in the late 1920's, in a scene worthy of Gatsby, several of the Round Table's diehard croquet fanatics fought off the falling darkness by driving their cars through the shrubbery to the perimeter of the course. In the cross-hatch of beams their headlights threw on the lawn, they played all night. [Dorothy] Parker watched a similar scene at the Swope estate from Ring Lardner's porch. 'Jesus Christ,' she said, 'the heirs to the ages.'"*
>
> From *Wit's End: Days and Nights of the Algonquin Round Table* by James R. Gaines

In the 1920s and 1930s, the citizens of Hollywood began playing croquet. This city, which was always searching for unusual entertainments, was delighted when Harpo Marx, whose interest in the game was so great that he converted an extra bedroom into an air-conditioned storage area for his equipment, introduced croquet to the movie capital. In no time at all, Sunday afternoon games at the homes of movie moguls Darryl Zanuck and Sam Goldwyn became very chic. It was said that Mr. Goldwyn particularly enjoyed the game as long as he won, and it was accepted etiquette that even if he came in the middle of a contest in progress, somehow or other he would finish victorious. The movie executives bid such stars as Tyrone Power, George Sanders, and Louis Jourdan (still a championship player today) to join in the games.

During the 1940s and 1950s, croquet once again faded out of the limelight. In the 1970s, the United States Croquet Association was formed by Jack Osborn to promote and regulate the sport of croquet, and the interest generated by the enthusiasm of this group has promoted a national reawakening to the fun and excitement of croquet.

Today the game once considered the exclusive province of the very rich has found its way into the backyards of suburbia and onto the lawns of the average American family.

In seventeenth-century France, when croquet was first gaining popularity, the Marquise de Sévigné, a remarkable lady of fashion whose more than one thousand letters give valuable insight into one of the most opulent courts in history, referred to the game as "un aimable jeu pour les personnes bien faites et adroites."

Today it is still a friendly game for clever and skillful people.

THE EQUIPMENT

The original equipment for croquet consisted of wickets made from bent willow branches and mallets created by attaching wooden heads to tree branches or broomsticks. As the game became popular the equipment was refined, but it wasn't until London toymaker John Jaques made the first complete set in the 1860s, called a croqueterie, that there was any uniformity to the tools for croquet. In the early 1870s, Milton Bradley of Springfield, Massachusetts, a printer whose press had broken down, causing him to search for another source of income, decided to market a croqueterie in an "elegant chestnut box." American sets at that time were very elaborate, comprising two posts (stakes), ten iron bridges (wickets), and four, six, or eight balls and the same number of mallets. The balls were ten inches in diameter and weighed about eight ounces. The width of the bridges was equal to the circumference of the ball. White was the suggested bridge color (as it is today) because it made the wickets stand out, and also, "contrasted more pleasingly with the green of the turf."

Other companies began making croquet sets and the equipment, although somewhat individual, was essentially constructed in the same manner. After the turn of the century, manufacturers began to modify the traditional designs, creating mallets in a variety of styles to give players an advantage on the court. The variations became so numerous and the game changed so dramatically that even the name was altered. Dropping the *c* and *t,* a new game, roque, was invented.

The alterations in the equipment led to confusion and even dissipated many of the skills and strategies required for traditional croquet, which led to a loss of some interest in the true game.

Fortunately, contemporary croquet players do not have to face these problems. Today the basic structure of the mallets and other equipment is relatively standardized; however, the materials and craftsmanship that go into the making of the equipment vary greatly in quality and substance.

The most elaborate croquet sets cost as much as sixteen hundred dollars, but you can get a complete collection of equipment for as little as twenty dollars. In the past, championship sets were the most expensive and were considered the finest available. However they can, due to their structure, increase the expertise necessary for the competition.

When considering the different types of croquet sets it is important to realize that, as the sport differs from the game, the championship sets differ from the simpler backyard variety. Obviously championship sets have the equipment necessary for championship play, which includes six wickets versus the traditional nine for a backyard game, and mallets that are often longer and heavier than backyard mallets. Championship sets constitute only about one percent of the almost three hundred thousand croquet sets sold every year.

It isn't necessary to invest in a championship set for a simple afternoon's entertainment. Backyard sets have become in recent years as elegant, extensive, and sometimes as expensive as the most elaborate of the championship sets. Fortunately for the budget-conscious croquet fan, there is a huge range of styles and excellent quality equipment between the very expensive and the very inexpensive. These sets, ranging in price from one hundred to five hundred dollars, have become the most popular as interest in the game grows anew.

The amount spent on a croquet set is a personal decision, but regardless of the price, it is helpful to have some knowledge of the basic equipment—mallets, balls, stakes, and wickets—before purchasing them.

EQUIPMENT
·
MALLETS

Although available in a variety of materials, the best mallets are made of ash or hickory, and most weigh between 1½ and 4 pounds. Mallet heads are rectangular, square, or round, between 6½ inches and 9 inches long, while the shafts vary in length from 24 to 36 inches. The shafts and heads of the mallets should be painted a solid color, or varnished with a colored stripe.

Very elegant mallets that come with the more expensive sets often have brass fittings around the head and leather handgrips. These fancy touches are not necessary for a backyard game, but regardless of the price of your equipment it is wise to take your individual mallet needs into consideration when choosing a croquet set, particularly the weight of the mallet and length of the mallet shaft.

For example, if you are especially tall, look for a set with the longest mallets. Or if you plan to play with children or mature adults, you might opt for a set with the lightest mallets.

Much like a tennis racquet or a golf club, croquet mallets can have a very personal quality. Before buying any set, hold the mallets in your hands, test the grip, and get the feel of them to see if they are right for you. Chances are, as you begin playing the game, one particular mallet will begin to be uniquely yours and become your favorite. Many players have a "lucky mallet," which they are convinced helps them make particularly difficult shots and win games.

BALLS

Balls for the backyard game are usually made of plastic or milled woods, 3 to 3⅝ inches in diameter, weighing 9 ounces to 1 pound. The balls can be solid color or varnished with a painted stripe.

STAKES

The stakes should also be made of wood, 18 inches high, with colored stripes, which indicate the order of play.

WICKETS

Wickets are one area in which, with little effort, your game can be adjusted to become more interesting and challenging. Many backyard croquet sets (particularly the inexpensive ones) come with wickets made of galvanized wire, much like a bent coat hanger, 4 to 6 inches wide. Wire wickets, although certainly functional, are not very substantial. And entering these wickets with the ball is relatively easy due to the wide aperture. Although this may sound good, since the object of the game is to make the wicket, if it's too simple the contest loses some of its interest.

Championship cast-iron wickets are solid and narrow structures that can cost as much as the total of the rest of your equipment. Championship wickets may weigh about 6

pounds each and require a certain amount of strength to place in the ground. These wickets can be as narrow as 3¾ inches wide, thus making entry very difficult. (Remember, the normal croquet ball is 3 to 3⅝ inches in diameter.)

There is another alternative: the challenge hoop, also called the winter wicket. If the usual wire wickets are too simple, and the championship wickets too difficult, then the winter wicket is a nice compromise. In fact, many of the better sets produced for backyard use now include winter wickets as standard equipment. The winter wickets are usually about 4 inches in width and made of substantial, but relatively light, wrought iron. Consequently they are strong enough to withstand heavy use, and the opening is small enough to make the game interesting. At the same time, the winter wicket is not so cumbersome or narrow as to make things too difficult. The weight, structure, and dimensions of the winter wicket make it a worthwhile investment for the interested player.

Three types of wickets: tournament, wire, and winter.

Having selected and purchased a croquet set, there are a few things to keep in mind about maintaining the equipment to make sure it remains in good condition and lasts a lifetime.

1. Never strike any ball other than the furnished croquet balls with the mallets.

2. Never use the mallets to drive the stakes into the ground.

3. Push the wickets into the ground with your hands. Using a hammer will chip the paint on some models or bend the wickets.

4. When finished playing, towel dry the mallets and balls. A thin coating of shellac or furniture polish will help protect them from rain and dampness.

5. When they are not in use, hang the mallets between two pegs or replace them in the stand provided with the set.

6. Always bring the equipment indoors after playing. Store in a cool, dry place, not a damp garage, to prevent warping.

ABOVE: **Measuring distance between wickets.**
BELOW: **Hammacher Schlemmer's elaborate croquet storage lounge.**

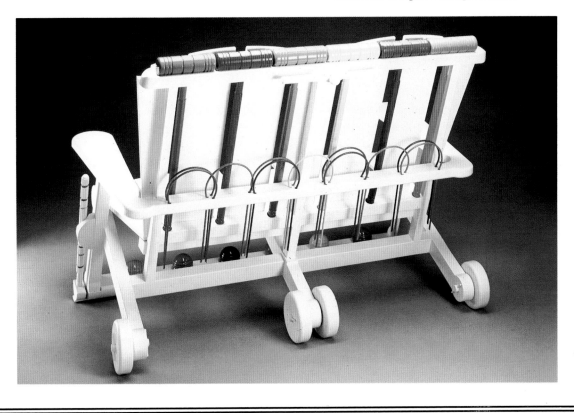

"Alice thought she had never seen such a curious croquet-ground in her life: it was all ridges and furrows; the croquet balls were live hedgehogs, and the mallets live flamingoes, and the soldiers had to double themselves up and stand on their hands and feet, to make the arches.

"The chief difficulty Alice found at first was in managing her flamingo: she succeeded in getting its body tucked away, comfortably enough under her arm, with its legs hanging down, but generally, just as she had got its neck nicely straightened out, and was going to give the hedgehog a blow with its head, it would twist itself round and look up into her face, with such a puzzled expression that she could not help bursting out laughing; and, when she had got its head down, and was going to begin again, it was very provoking to find that the hedgehog had unrolled itself, and was in the act of crawling away: besides all this, there was generally a ridge or a furrow in the way wherever she wanted to send the hedgehog to, and, as the doubled-up soldiers were always getting up and walking off to other parts of the ground, Alice soon came to the conclusion that it was a very difficult game indeed.

"The players all played at once without waiting for turns, quarrelling all the while, and fighting for the hedgehogs: and in a very short time the Queen was in a furious passion, and went stamping about, and shouting 'Off with his head!' or 'Off with her head!' about once in a minute."

From *Alice's Adventures in Wonderland* by Lewis Carroll

COURTS

•

Avid croquet players have been known to spend up to fifty thousand dollars creating the proper lawn on which to play the game. This sum includes sterilizing the grass to kill weeds, installing a proper drainage system, and bulldozing the area to levelness. Lawn furniture is additional. Needless to say, it's unlikely that many weekend players will invest this heavily in a croquet court. However, regardless of the quality of your lawn, it is important that the grass be as short as possible. While the game can be played on an uncut lawn, long grass forces players to push their shots and risk losing accuracy.

Although it is not necessary to have a great grassy expanse such as belonged to the massive estates of the gilded age, a certain

Accuracy is important when measuring the croquet court.

amount of space *is* required to play croquet. The ideal backyard court is fifty feet wide and one hundred feet long. These specifications can be scaled down, depending on available space, to as little as ten by twenty feet, although thirty by sixty feet is perhaps the smallest croquet court size to offer interesting play. The charts on pages 86–88 indicate how to properly lay out a full-sized and two reduced-sized courts, along with the correct placement and distances between wickets and stakes. When creating a court, adjust the size simply by keeping the width of the playing area half the length, and place the stakes and wickets accordingly.

A perfectly rectangular lawn is not a requirement. In fact, trees, shrubs, or other natural hazards can actually add interest to the game. The court can be laid out at angles around the house or other obstacles. (When one really gets into croquet, the house can suddenly be considered an obstacle.) The chart on page 89 illustrates the proper method of setting up a court at an angle. As long as the basic relative distances are maintained, the arrangement of the court can vary as required.

The correct placement of the stakes and wickets is also very straightforward. Based on the one-hundred-by-fifty-foot court, the two stakes are placed at each end of the court, six feet from the boundary line. The first and seventh wickets are twelve feet from the closest end line, and the second and sixth wickets are eighteen feet from the closest end line. The fourth wicket is placed at the center of the court while the outside wickets, third, fifth, tenth, and twelfth, are placed thirty-four feet from the end line and six feet from the side boundary line. These placements are adjusted with the size of the court.

PLAYING THE
GAME

The object of croquet is to complete the course of wickets and hit the finishing stake before your opponents do.

There are four basic versions of the game:

1. *Individual.* Two to six players (depending on the extent of the equipment) each play one ball.

2. *Singles.* Two players play two balls.

3. *Doubles.* Four players (in teams of two) each play one ball.

4. *Triples.* Six players (in teams of three) each play one ball.

Order of play is determined by the order of the colored stripes on the stakes.

Regardless of the arrangement of play, a ball scores a wicket by passing through that wicket. However, there are comprehensive rules governing the manner and means by which a player may enter a wicket, and these are detailed in the rules section of this book.

At this point it is advantageous for beginners to study and master the vocabulary of croquet. This will not only be useful in understanding the rules and helpful in comprehending the various strategies and shots outlined in this chapter but will also make the individual who has memorized the language sound particularly intelligent and well informed. The following terms are important for the serious, or even casual, croquet player.

A CROQUET GLOSSARY

•

Alive A player's ball is alive if it has cleared a wicket. This procedure enables it to play on all other balls.

All-around break The sign of a very skilled (or very lucky) player, this term describes a player who makes all of the wickets in a single turn.

Approach shot This is the process by which a player places a ball in such a position as to clear the next wicket, or roquet another ball.

Ball-in-hand A ball that for any reason (e.g., going out of bounds or hitting another ball illegally) must be picked up and moved.

Bisque Allowing a player to replay a shot from the spot where it was originally taken. This process of giving an extra stroke to a weaker player acts as a handicap to help equalize a game.

Clearing Becoming alive by making a wicket.

Continuation shot The extra stroke earned by either clearing a wicket or taking croquet on another ball.

Croquet shot The shot taken after a player roquets (see meaning below) another's ball. The player places his ball next to the roqueted ball and strikes his ball with the

mallet, driving the roqueted ball in any direction. The player may also place a hand or foot on his ball before striking his ball with the mallet, driving the roqueted ball away.

Deadness A player who has roqueted another ball is "dead" on that ball and cannot play off it until his ball clears the next wicket.

Double tap A player accidentally hitting his own ball twice in one stroke. This is a fault.

Double target A situation in which two balls are placed so close together that the striker's target area is, in effect, doubled.

Drive shot A player hitting squarely on his ball when taking a croquet shot, causing the roqueted ball to go much farther than the striker's ball.

Fault An unacceptable stroke or action that results in a penalty.

Foot shot Taking a croquet shot with the striker's foot on his own ball.

Jaws The entrance to the wickets.

Join up Playing a ball close to a partner's ball.

Jump shot Striking the ball so that it leaves the ground, avoiding a blocking ball, wicket, or stake.

Leave The positions in which a player leaves his and his opponents' balls at the end of his turn.

Out-of-bounds A ball that is more than halfway across the boundary line.

Pass To pass up a turn.

Pass roll A croquet shot that sends the striker's ball farther than the roqueted ball.

Peel Causing another player's ball to make its next wicket.

Peg-out The last shot of a game in which the ball scores the peg or stake point.

Push A stroke form that may be used only when making a croquet shot. In this stroke, the head of the player's mallet remains on the ball after hitting it.

Roll shot A croquet shot in which both the player's ball and the roqueted ball travel along the same line.

Roquet A move in which a player's ball comes into contact with another's ball, either intentionally or unintentionally. The player making this shot is entitled either to two additional strokes or to roquet or croquet the ball hit and then take one additional stroke.

Roquet-croquet A croquet shot in which the hand or foot is not placed on the opponent's ball.

Rover A player whose ball has made the last wicket. However, instead of hitting the stake, the player prefers to continue play, making his ball a rover. Balls that hit the final stake are not allowed to be rovers.

Rush A roquet shot that sends the roqueted ball to a preplanned position.

Split shot A shot that sends the player's and the roqueted balls in different directions.

Stake-out The last shot of the game when a ball scores the stake point.

Sticky wicket An unusually tight wicket, difficult to clear without getting stuck.

Stop-shot A shot in which the roqueted ball goes much farther than the player's ball.

Striker The player whose turn it is.

Stroke The process of hitting the ball, whether the strike is successful or not.

Take-off shot A shot in which the roqueted ball moves only a short distance and the player's ball moves a longer distance.

Time limit This may be suggested to maintain play between shots (forty-five seconds, for example) or actually limit the length of the contest.

Wicket An arch through which the ball must pass.

GRIPS

•

It is possible to hold the mallet in a particularly individual manner. But in order to get maximum dexterity and control out of each strike, it is a good idea to experiment and practice with the standard grips until you are able to make one of them your own. Comfort and personal choice, of course, have a lot to do with choosing a grip, but in backyard play, your grip will be influenced by the length of the mallet handle. If you are playing with a short-handled, inexpensive mallet, the way you position your hands will be different than if you are holding a longer-handled mallet. Some of the basic grips can be awkward if the mallet is very short. But at least one of the following hand positions in which it is correct to hold a croquet mallet will be functional and comfortable for almost everyone. Of course, your grip can be adjusted or changed according to the shot you're taking.

THE STANDARD BRITISH GRIP

This grip is similar to the American except that the hands are close together rather than wide apart. The finger positions are identical to those in the American grip.

THE IRISH GRIP

This grip is very helpful in balancing the strength of a player's two hands. In some grips it is possible for the stronger hand to exert too much influence on the stroke and thus cause the ball to veer off in one direction or the other. The Irish grip is effective in preventing this because both hands cup the mallet with palms facing away from the body and thumbs resting on the shaft. Incidentally, this grip was popular with championship players during the Edwardian era, and today offers excellent accuracy with short-handled mallets.

THE STANDARD AMERICAN GRIP

Grip the top of the mallet with one hand and place the other six to twelve inches below. The fingers of the top hand are wrapped around the mallet while the fingers of the bottom are separated, the index finger pointed down the side or back of the mallet.

THE OSBORN GRIP

This grip was created by the United States Croquet Association president, Jack Osborn. In it, the thumb of the top hand is placed against the back of the handle, securing the hand. The other hand is placed directly beneath, with the forefinger extended down the shaft of the mallet. This is a very secure grip, offering maximum control over the mallet.

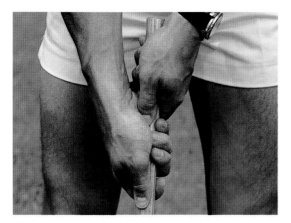

THE GOLF GRIP

This grip is a favorite with many backyard players, particularly those who play golf. It is similar to the Irish grip, in that both palms are cupped around the shaft facing each other and both thumbs rest on the top of the shaft. The difference between the grips is that in the golf grip the left thumb is covered by the right.

STANCES
•

Like your grip, your stance when approaching the ball will have a definite effect on the accuracy and distance your strike achieves.

THE CENTER STANCE

The player stands directly behind the ball, moving the mallet between his legs as it strikes the ball. This is the traditional croquet stance and is considered the most effective position for guiding and controlling each shot. Although it may take some practice to get used to, this stance will add control to your game. If you feel awkward in the center stance, you can adjust it for comfort by placing one foot slightly in front of the other (about six to eighteen inches) and shifting the majority of your weight to the forward foot. The distance between your feet depends on personal comfort.

THE SIDE STANCE

Ladies at the turn of the century used this stance because wearing long dresses made it impossible for them to swing the mallet between their legs. It remains useful for those who have trouble adjusting their bodies to the other stances. This position can be particularly helpful to someone with a physical infirmity such as a bad back that restricts movement. To assume the side stance, bend the knees, face the ball, and hold the mallet to the side of either foot, thus swinging the mallet along the side of the body rather than in front of or between the legs.

> "*Keep your temper* and remember when your turn comes."
> From *Croquet: Its Principles and Rules*
> by A. Rover
> Milton Bradley and Co., 1871

THE GOLF STANCE

Like the golf grip, this is the most natural way for many backyard players to stand. The feet are shoulder-width apart and the mallet is centered for impact with the ball at the center point between the feet. The body is held almost exactly as it is when approaching a golf tee. This stance is excellent for long shots or for use in high grass or on an uneven lawn.

SWING
•

After selecting a grip and a stance, your next step to playing good croquet is accomplishing an effective swing. There is nothing secret or difficult about swinging the croquet mallet. Simply put, you should move the mallet with an easy and comfortable swing, allowing your *arms,* not your torso or hips, to lead the movement of the mallet.

To make a wicket, draw an imaginary line between your ball and the wicket, concentrating your attention on the wicket.

Approach the ball and strike it squarely in the center using enough force to drive the ball completely through the wicket.

Follow the strike through with your mallet, keeping your concentration on the wicket opening.

The height to which you lift the mallet will affect the strength of your shot: A short backswing will have less force and result in less ground being covered by the ball, while a high backswing will increase the force of your strike and make the ball travel farther. In general, your backswing should be slow. Do not rush the strike or you can lose accuracy. Also, it is unnecessary to perform a great sweeping action in order to make a good strike. Relax, let your arms do the work, and follow through.

As discussed previously, the position of your body influences your shot. And it also influences your swing. Placing your body too far from the ball can cause you to hit the ball during the upswing of your mallet, resulting in the ball having a limited roll. Placing your body too close to the ball can cause you to hit the ball on your downswing, making the ball jump.

To hit the ball squarely in the center, you should position your body so that the mallet strikes the ball at the lowest part of your swing.

STRIKES

•

There are many situations during play when, rather than making just a straight-across-the-court shot, you want to direct your ball toward a particular position. Several shots can help you achieve this versatility.

Croquet strikes fall into two categories: single and double shots. With the single shot you strike only your own ball in an effort to hit an opponent's ball, avoid an opponent's ball, or make a wicket. These are the basic moves. There are other single shots that are designed not only to hit an opponent's ball but to send it in a different direction, but these are somewhat complicated and better suited to the sport rather than the game.

Double shots are used after you have roqueted your opponent's ball and want to croquet it and improve your own position.

SINGLE SHOTS

For backyard croquet with your family and friends you should master three basic single shots: the roquet, making a wicket, and the jump.

The Roquet The roquet shot is the strike you take after you track down your opponent's ball and have it in your sights. Roquet is the actual hitting of your opponent's ball with yours so that you can take croquet on it, sending your opponent's ball "up the river," or giving yourself extra shots.

To make the roquet shot, you must stalk your opponent's ball. Begin by drawing an imaginary line through the center of both your ball and your opponent's. Then extend the line back to your body, holding your mallet out in front of you, above your ball, lining up the shot.

Position your body properly and then slowly swing the mallet, keeping your eye on *your* ball and hitting it at the bottom of your swing. If you have completed the process correctly, your ball should travel across the court and hit your opponent's ball.

If you continually miss roquet shots, check all of the elements. Make sure you are taking enough time to align the shot properly and that your stance is correct for hitting your ball directly in the center.

Making a Wicket Making a wicket is one of the most exciting parts of the game. Not only does it permit a player to gain extra shots, it also gives him a feeling of accom-

Lining up the croquet shot.

**No matter how far the ball must travel,
proper form is the key to making a wicket.**

plishment, like hitting a home run or scoring a basket. However, it is too often possible to be directly in front of a wicket, swing the mallet, and stare as the ball gently slides off to one side, which not only leaves the player feeling rather foolish, but results in having to take additional shots in order to get back in position to try it again.

To make a wicket, simply focus your concentration on the *opening* of the wicket rather than on your ball, and strike your ball in the center. Carry through with your swing as if you want the head of the mallet to follow the ball through the wicket.

Do not strike the ball so lightly that it travels up to the wicket and then stops, or so hard that you lose control of the shot and the ball flies away from the wicket. Skill at making wickets can be attained only with practice.

The Jump Shot The jump shot is perhaps one of the most flamboyant croquet acts. In a game that relies on skill rather than grandstand plays, this is one move by which a player can elicit cheers from the bystanders.

The jump shot is used when you want to avoid hitting another ball that lies in your path. For example, if you're "dead" on an opponent's ball and it is in your way, you can employ the jump shot to reach your desired position.

In tournament play, the jump shot is most often accomplished using the center stance, in which the mallet is swung between the legs. If you recall, standing too close to your ball when striking will make it jump rather than roll, which is precisely what you want it to do in this instance. Position yourself literally over your ball, with your insteps parallel to the ball. Grip the mallet securely with both hands low on the shaft and aim at the top third of the ball, preparing to hit down. Swing the mallet back and make contact with the ball as the mallet is in the down movement of your swing. If hit properly the ball will jump over any obstruction you are trying to avoid and sail into position on the other side.

You don't want to actually hit the ground with the mallet head, although during your first few tries it is likely that you will. Also, it is a wise idea to practice this move alone because, until you master it, too much strength behind your swing can result in your ball lifting not only over your opponent's ball, but possibly over your opponent as well. Control is very important in the jump shot.

The backyard player accustomed to using the golf stance will find that, by adjusting his position, he can complete a successful jump shot.

DOUBLE SHOTS

The double shots are used after a player has roqueted his opponent's ball.

There is something almost terrifying about the gruesome glee with which even the most mild-mannered individual will joyfully croquet his nearest and dearest. The traditional method of taking croquet is to set the two balls together (after having roqueted your opponent) and then, placing your foot or hand on your ball, strike your ball with the intention of sending your opponent's ball off into the bushes. And if you can't resist this procedure, your game is pretty well set. However, with a little imagination and creativity, you can take croquet on your opponent's ball in ways that will give you valuable opportunities to advance your own ball.

Obviously, if you put your foot on your ball when taking croquet, it cannot move at all; consequently you haven't aided your position, but rather simply lessened your opponent's. If you really want to become an adroit croquet player, you will forget all about the traditional foot maneuver and concentrate on making a croquet move that will enhance your

To take croquet, place your ball tightly against your opponent's.

position on the court as much as punish your opponent, if not more.

The best way to do this is by mastering the strokes that will not only place your ball where you want it after taking croquet but also place your opponent's ball in a position where it will be useful to you again.

It is also important to give up the option of placing your ball a croquet mallet's head away from the roqueted ball and taking two strokes. Although this move is an allowable alternative to taking croquet, it doesn't give you the advantage that a good croquet strike will provide.

To really play well, *take croquet,* and do it as professionally as possible. When completing any of the following moves to accomplish

"We predict for croquet a success wider in this [country, America] than it has reached in any other country. When we work or fight, we work and fight harder than any other people, and we should be as enthusiastic in our play."
From *Croquet: Its Principles and Rules*
by A. Rover
Milton Bradley and Co., 1871

good croquet, it is vital to remember always that when taking croquet, *your ball must be placed directly against your opponent's.* If the balls are not tightly together, you will not be able to complete the shot you're trying to make accurately.

As with the single shots, there are some very sophisticated possibilities in taking croquet. However, for backyard purposes, there are five shots you should learn: three strikes that control the distance covered by both your and your opponent's balls; a split shot, useful when you want to send your ball in one direction and your opponent's in another; and a wicket approach split shot, helpful if you need to remove an opponent's ball from between your ball and the opening of a wicket.

The three important shots that govern distance are the stop shot, the roll shot, and the drive.

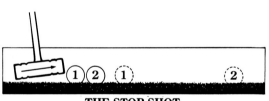

THE STOP SHOT

The Stop Shot This strike causes your opponent's ball to travel farther than your own.

Place both balls as close together as possible and stand about one step farther back from your ball than usual. Swing the mallet forward, jamming the heel (back end) of the mallet head into the ground as the front end of the mallet hits your ball. *Do not follow through with your swing.* Stopping your swing upon contact with your ball will effectively cause all of the force of the strike to be concentrated on your opponent's ball, sending it a long distance while moving yours only a short way.

THE ROLL SHOT

The Roll Shot This strike will move both your ball and your opponent's approximately the same distance.

Place both balls tightly together and take a stance with your feet apart, one behind the ball, the other extended back. Place your weight on the forward foot and bend your body forward. Aim at your ball and use a short backswing, making contact with your ball on the downswing, being sure you carry through with your swing.

This is not a simple shot and can, if done improperly, result in hitting your ball twice or even more (a fault). Aim carefully and take your time, particularly with your swing.

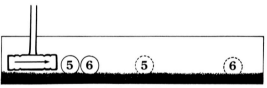

THE DRIVE SHOT

The Drive Shot Considered the backbone of croquet shots, this strike will move both your ball and your opponent's a considerable distance, with your opponent's ball traveling about three times as far as yours. Consequently, you can send your ball a long way (and your opponent's even farther) depending on the strength of your swing.

The drive shot is actually rather easy to accomplish because you approach and strike your ball as if there simply weren't any obstacle in your way. The amount of energy you put in your swing will determine the distance both balls travel.

Place the balls together. Use your usual stance and grip and take a slow backswing. Swing cleanly toward your ball, making contact at the bottom of your swing, and follow through. Remember, the height of the backswing determines the force of the shot. Carry through as if your opponent's ball didn't exist.

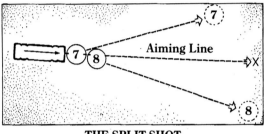

THE SPLIT SHOT

The Split Shot This is an important move if you want to be a good croquet player. Once you have roqueted your opponent's ball you may find that you need to drive your ball to one side while sending his off to the other, and the split will accomplish this somewhat intricate maneuver. If you are really expert, you can even place your opponent's ball in a particular place where you can take advantage of it later or where your partner can make use of it.

In the diagram, the player wants to place his ball (7) to the left and send his opponent's ball (8) to the right. To complete this task, the player places his ball directly behind his opponent's and then creates three imaginary lines: one in the direction he wants the opponent's ball to go, one for the direction of his own, and a line between the two. Having lined up the shot, the player then aims directly for the line between the two (X). Never aim in the direction you want your ball to travel as this will probably result in neither ball doing what you want. Using your usual stance and grip, swing the mallet with the force necessary to send the balls the distance you want them to move.

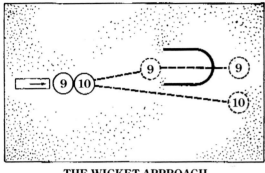

**THE WICKET APPROACH
SPLIT SHOT**

The Wicket Approach Split Shot This strike is valuable when not only the separation of the balls is necessary, but the final destination of each is important.

The diagram shows the player's ball (9) ending up at a point ready to enter a wicket, while the opponent's ball (10) is placed where it could be used to roquet again after the player has shot the wicket, or, if the player chooses to go in a different direction or complete the game, be vulnerable to the player's partner.

When taking a split shot to prepare your ball to make a wicket, the lining-up procedures are the same as for the usual split shot. However, the amount of force and the type of distance shot are very important. The stop, roll, or drive shots can be used in a break situation, thus combining the benefits of moving an opponent's ball out of the way and placing it where you want it with the advantage of controlling the distance both balls travel. Depending on the distance your ball needs to travel to reach the wicket, choose the distance strike that will put your ball directly in front of the wicket when the move is completed.

ETIQUETTE

•

Depending on how you look at it, the disappearance of the times when croquet etiquette included the warning that ladies should not stroll across the courts, moving the balls about with their long skirts, can be either good or bad. But despite the lack of formality to contemporary backyard games, there are still rules of polite and correct behavior that should be maintained during a croquet match.

Players should play their strokes as quickly as possible. After all, it becomes somewhat dull for others to have to stand by and wait while a particularly meticulous player examines every angle and outcome of each stroke. A minute is enough, although in some contests a forty-five-second time limit may be imposed.

Players should never stand in an opponent's sight lines. This is self-explanatory and is really only good manners.

A player may not take advice or instruc-

"The ladies will very much oblige all their associates in croquet by avoiding long dresses, which are continually dragging the balls about over the ground greatly to the annoyance of the players and disturbance of the game."

From *Croquet: Its Principles and Rules*
by A. Rover
Milton Bradley and Co., 1871

tions from another player or spectator other than his doubles partner. Of course, in some friendly games everyone offers advice to all players. But if you want to maintain a good relationship with your friends, chances are you should act on your own.

When a player notices that an unacceptable stroke is about to be taken, he may suggest a referee be called. This rule is clearly for matches in which the players are trying to maintain a strict adherence to the rules and regulations. For your backyard contest, you may not think illegal strikes are particularly important, but ignoring illegal shots (or trying to get away with them yourself) suggests cheating. And chances are if one player begins to slip improper moves into the game and isn't stopped, the other players will join in, and any semblance of organization will disappear.

GOLF CROQUET

•

Golf croquet is a variation of the basic croquet game, played worldwide, that can be enjoyable and interesting for a large group of people. It is somewhat simpler than regular croquet and does not offer or require some of the difficult and sophisticated moves of "real" croquet. Golf croquet is also a good way to

practice basic croquet shots. It can be learned quickly and be played in less time than a regular croquet game. It is interesting to note that the word *croquet* in the title of the game is actually a misnomer because the croquet shot itself is never used in golf croquet.

Golf croquet can be played with either six or nine wickets by two, four, or six players in teams. Like the real game of golf, all of the players are attempting to make the same wicket at the same time. However, like croquet (and unlike golf), the balls are permitted to interfere with one another.

Wickets are given point values, and a point is scored when a team completes a wicket with either of its balls. The balls are played in the same sequence as regular croquet, according to the color bands on the stakes. But unlike croquet, there are no extra shots or turns. Once a color, blue for example, has made a wicket, all the players then proceed to the next wicket and the next color, red, has the first shot at it.

It should be noted that some of the interesting aspects of real croquet, including the jump shot, are not allowed in golf croquet. And although the croquet shot is not used either, it is possible for a player to use his ball to displace his opponent's. Also, in golf croquet, if a player's ball starts to enter a wicket but does not completely pass through the jaws, the player must wait for his next turn and then knock it back out and try to reenter on his following turn. However, a player's ball can score the wicket by being pushed through the wicket by an opponent's ball.

These are just a few of the interesting aspects of golf croquet. It can be a good family game and has become increasingly popular over the past few years. The rules for golf croquet follow the rules for croquet on page 85.

THE
SOCIAL SCENE

roquet has always been a remarkably social game, played by groups of people gathering together for an afternoon of pleasure and enjoyment. It is, of course, possible to say the same for touch football, but such sports require a greater effort than many people are willing to invest in a casual pastime. Besides, croquet *lends* itself to entertaining friends so easily. Spectators can lounge comfortably along the sidelines and comment on the quality of play, without hav-

ing to move around to avoid missing anything (or being hit). And players not actively engaged in making a strike can catch up on the latest news or gossip from their partners, or, in a friendly game, their opponents.

During croquet's heyday in the 1850s, croquet parties were held often and considered major social events. With as many as one hundred guests, the game would begin in the late afternoon and the contest would be accompanied by an imported orchestra, subtly sequestered away from the court. Following the game, guests would indulge in a champagne supper and dance until late in the evening. Obviously, these people knew how to play croquet.

Even today, when the United States Croquet Association gathers for tournaments, the contests are highlighted by elegant entertainments such as the Croquet Ball. Photographs of the party show players attending in evening clothes and sneakers, an appropriate combination illustrating the aura of civilized sport.

Although you may not have the space (or even the desire) for an orchestra or a formal ball in your backyard, you will find that croquet still offers wonderful entertaining possibilities. A croquet party is a perfect backdrop for a country picnic, an elegant luncheon, or an afternoon tea.

THE WELL-DRESSED CROQUET PLAYER

•

Often, when a department store or advertiser wishes to indicate that a particular item is classic or chic, they will place a croquet mallet in the hands of the mannequins or models. Even during croquet's golden age, fashion magazines would inform ladies of the latest in sporting costumes. Above the coy caption *pour le sport* would appear illustrations of various garments deemed appropriate for the croquet game in polite society.

The move to all-white clothing came after the turn of the century and, at least as far as sport tournaments go, is still the required color under United States Croquet Association rules. But even this traditional group has relaxed somewhat in the past few years. Whereas dresses, white flannels, and long-

sleeve shirts were the only way to appear at one time, today you will find contestants in shorts and polo shirts. These garments are, of course, still white.

In the backyard, what you wear is your own business. But aside from adding a unique touch to your game, the right costume can actually contribute to your performance on the court.

Loose, light clothing makes movement easier. And sneakers or soft-soled shoes are vital for mobility and traction on the lawn. No Victorian lady would have thought of going into the sun without a hat to protect her skin, and owing to tradition as well as for convenience and comfort, hats and sunshades are still an integral part of basic croquet clothing.

Practical considerations aside, just as the croquet court itself can evoke the romance and nostalgia of more elegant times, wearing something special can add to the style and charm of playing the game.

AFTERNOON TEA

(for 4)

Tea Sandwiches:

Cucumber   Watercress

Chicken

Egg and Tomato

•

Buttermilk Scones

Banana Bread

Marmalade   Jams

•

Fresh Fruits

Darjeeling Tea

AFTERNOON TEA

•

Anna, Duchess of Bedford, popularized at-home tea parties in about 1860. The idea caught on immediately, and the tea party has been a staple of English social life ever since.

When croquet first came to the United States, tea parties were an important part of daily social intercourse. And during the summer months at country estates, tea was held outside. Those must have been beautiful occasions. Damask-covered tables set with massive silver tea sets, polished and catching the glint of the fading sun, were surrounded by exquisite arrangements of delicious food.

Today, tea parties in America are experiencing a lavish renaissance, much like the game of croquet. And the two are uniquely compatible.

The tea table, gracefully set, should be placed in a shady spot in view of the croquet court, and the meal can be served either before or after the game.

Afternoon tea continues to be one of the most charming and dignified of gatherings. And though perhaps over the years the gild-ing has faded slightly, the elegance of this particularly pleasant and gentle entertainment remains.

•

TEA SANDWICHES

1 loaf white sandwich bread, thinly sliced
1 loaf whole-wheat sandwich bread, thinly sliced

SANDWICH BUTTER
1 stick unsalted butter, softened
½ cup mayonnaise
Salt, white pepper, and cayenne to taste

Combine all ingredients in food processor and blend until smooth.

CUCUMBER

1. Peel one seedless cucumber and split it lengthwise. Scoop out the core.

2. Thinly slice the cucumber, sprinkle lightly with salt, and let the slices drain in a colander for 30 minutes.

3. Spread the sandwich butter on slices of white bread. Roll the cucumber slices in a dry towel to squeeze out any excess moisture.

4. Gently place the cucumber on one side of the buttered bread, then top with another slice of buttered bread. Trim the crusts and cut in half diagonally.

WATERCRESS

1. Spread slices of white bread with the sandwich butter. Wash and coarsely chop the leaves of one bunch of watercress, sprinkle them lightly on the buttered bread, and top with another slice of buttered bread. Trim the crusts and cut in half diagonally.

> *"There were teas for. . . happy occasions—in particular those put on to add to the enjoyment of summer sports. The tennis tea was an essential part of country life, as were croquet and cricket teas. Those served at Henley, Hurlingham, the Eton and Harrow match and, later, Wimbledon, were an essential part of the London season."*
> From *The National Trust and The West Country Tourist Board's Book of Afternoon Tea* by Marika Hanbury Tenison

CHICKEN

1. Cut one poached or baked boneless chicken breast into large cubes. Place the cubes in a food processor and chop.

2. Add 2 tablespoons of mayonnaise, a pinch of salt, white pepper, and a grating of nutmeg. Blend until smooth.

3. Prepare sandwiches with chicken and whole-wheat bread. Trim the crusts and cut in half diagonally.

EGG AND TOMATO

1. Place one hard-cooked egg and one tablespoon of mayonnaise in the food processor and blend well. Season to taste with salt and white pepper.

2. Make sandwiches using whole-wheat bread, egg salad, and thin slices of tomato. Trim the crusts and cut in half diagonally.

● BANANA BREAD

⅓ cup (⅝ stick) unsalted butter
⅔ cup sugar
2 large eggs lightly beaten
1 cup (2 to 3) mashed ripe bananas
1¾ cups sifted all-purpose flour
2 teaspoons baking powder
¼ teaspoon baking soda
½ teaspoon salt
¼ cup coarsely chopped walnuts

1. Preheat oven to 350° F.

2. With an electric mixer, cream together the butter and sugar. Add the eggs and mix until light and fluffy. Add the mashed bananas and mix well. Add the flour, baking powder,

baking soda, and salt, beat until smooth, and fold in the nuts.

3. Pour into a prepared loaf pan and bake for 1 hour, or until a tester inserted in the center comes out clean. Cool in the pan for 10 minutes, remove and cool on a rack.

● BUTTERMILK SCONES

2 cups all-purpose flour
2 tablespoons sugar
½ teaspoon salt
2 teaspoons baking powder
3 tablespoons unsalted butter, softened
¼ cup currants
⅔ cup buttermilk

1. Preheat the oven to 425° F.

2. Sift together the flour, sugar, salt, and baking powder. Work in the butter until the mixture is coarse and pealike. Mix in the currants. Add the buttermilk and work into a soft dough.

3. On a floured board roll out the dough to a ½-inch thickness, and cut into triangles, diamond shapes, or 2-inch squares. Bake on a greased baking sheet pan for 12 to 15 minutes, until browned. Serve with butter, marmalade, or jam.

A FRENCH COUNTRY PICNIC

(for 8)

Country-style Pâté

Assorted Cheeses

•

Roast Leg of Lamb

Ratatouille

Flageolets Salad

Green Salad Vinaigrette

Assorted Breads

•

Strawberries with Crème Frâiche

Wine

A FRENCH COUNTRY PICNIC

•

Croquet was created in France, where outdoor dining virtually reached the level of an art form.

When Marie Antoinette decided to simplify her opulent existence, she chose to create a perfect paradise at her Petite Trianon. In this country area, she ordered that a small forest with artificial ponds be built. Here, the queen and her court played at games and donned clothes such as those worn by rustics or villagers, replacing their elegant silks and satins with modest muslins and large straw hats tied at the neck with ribbons. In their peasant costumes, the aristocracy moved gracefully over the perfectly trimmed lawns, flirting, nibbling strawberries, and congratulating themselves on their lack of sophistication.

An elegant picnic is an ideal backdrop for an afternoon of croquet. A romantic occasion for two, a large gathering for friends, or a special outing for the family are all enhanced by china, crystal, linen tablecloths and napkins, and, of course, a croquet contest.

Choose a quiet location under a flowering tree, toss a soft, old quilt over a grassy area, lavishly spread the food out, and enjoy an afternoon of croquet.

•

ROAST LEG OF LAMB

Served at room temperature with Dijon-style mustard and crusty French bread, this roast leg of lamb is perfect picnic fare. Taking the roast on a picnic requires a little planning—just bring along a big serving platter and a carving knife and fork.

1 5-pound leg of lamb, bone in and tied
4 garlic cloves, peeled and cut into slivers
2 tablespoons coarse salt
1 tablespoon freshly ground black pepper

1. Preheat the oven to 400° F.

2. With the point of a paring knife, make 1-inch-deep incisions in the lamb and insert the garlic slivers. Rub the lamb with salt and pepper.

3. Roast for approximately 1½ hours for rare meat, longer if you prefer it less pink. Allow the roast to sit for 15 to 30 minutes before carving. The roast can be prepared ahead of time, refrigerated, and then brought back to room temperature.

•

FLAGEOLETS SALAD

Flageolets, small greenish-white beans, are the traditional accompaniment to leg of lamb.

2 8-ounce cans flageolets
2 red onions, peeled and cut into thin slivers
1 head fennel, cut into thin slivers; include
    the leafy tops
1½ cups extra-virgin olive oil
½ cup red wine vinegar
Salt
Freshly ground black pepper

1. Drain the flageolets and place them in a large mixing bowl. Add the red onions and fennel and toss.

2. In a small bowl, mix the remaining ingredients for the dressing. Toss well with the vegetables. Add salt and pepper to taste.

RATATOUILLE

2 large eggplants
4 red peppers
2 large onions
2 zucchini
2 yellow squash
1 cup olive oil
1 tablespoon herbs de Provence
1 tablespoon salt
1 teaspoon freshly ground black pepper
6 garlic cloves, minced
3 bay leaves
8 fresh tomatoes, peeled and cut into wedges

1. Preheat the oven to 500° F.

2. Cut the eggplants, red peppers, onions, zucchini, and squash into strips approximately 2½″ x ¼″ x ¼″ in size. In a large bowl, toss the vegetables gently with ½ cup olive oil, herbs, salt, and pepper.

3. Spread the vegetables in one layer in a large flat baking pan, and bake for 20 minutes.

4. In a large pot heat the remaining ½ cup olive oil. Add the garlic and bay leaves, and sauté for 30 seconds. Add the tomatoes and cook for another minute or two.

5. Remove the roasted vegetables and add them to the tomato mixture, tossing well. This will keep in the refrigerator for several days, but always serve at room temperature.

"THINGS NOT TO BE FORGOTTEN AT A PICNIC

"A stick of horseradish, a bottle of mint-sauce well corked, a bottle of salad dressing, a bottle of vinegar, made mustard, pepper, salt, good oil, and pounded sugar. If it can be managed, take a little ice. It is scarcely necessary to say that plates, tumblers, wine-glasses, knives, forks, and spoons, must not be forgotten; as also teacups and saucers, 3 or 4 teapots, some lump sugar, and milk, if this last-named article cannot be obtained in the neighbourhood. Take 3 corkscrews. Beverages—3 dozen quart bottles of ale, packed in hampers; ginger-beer, soda-water, and lemonade, of each 2 dozen bottles; 6 bottles of sherry, 6 bottles of claret, champagne a discretion, and any other light wine that may be preferred, and 2 bottles of brandy. Water can usually be obtained so it is useless to take it."

From *Beeton's Book of Household Management*, 1861

GREEN SALAD VINAIGRETTE

1 head bibb lettuce
1 bunch watercress
2 bunches Belgian endive
¼ cup red wine vinegar
1 tablespoon Dijon-style mustard
1 teaspoon salt
½ teaspoon white pepper
½ cup peanut or soybean oil
¼ cup extra-virgin olive oil

1. Cut, wash, and spin dry all greens and place in a salad bowl.

2. Combine the vinegar, mustard, salt, and pepper in a small mixing bowl and blend with a fork or a wire whisk. Drizzle in the oils while beating continuously with whisk. Toss with the salad just before serving.

BUFFET LUNCHEON

(for 6)

*Asparagus with Balsamic
Vinaigrette*

•

Poached Salmon with Herb Sauce

Three-Grain Rice Salad

*Bibb, Watercress, and Tomato
Salad*

Country Rolls

•

Assorted Fruit Tarts

Chilled White Wine

•

A bright, sunny day and good friends are a wonderful combination. Add beautifully prepared food, and a perfect time follows naturally. For the busy host or hostess, a buffet can be one of the nicest and most convenient methods of doing a large party. Combining luncheon with croquet is an excellent way of taking full advantage of both the sunshine and the game. It can be an all-day event.

Of course, the presentation of the food is very important. And because croquet is rather romantic, it is nice to use antique china set on a polished wooden table to create the appropriate atmosphere. Placing the food outdoors will probably increase everyone's appetites, so plan plenty of simple, hearty fare. Save dessert until the competition is over and serve with champagne to toast the winners.

ASPARAGUS WITH BALSAMIC VINAIGRETTE

2 pounds asparagus, peeled and trimmed
2 tablespoons balsamic vinegar
1 teaspoon Dijon-style mustard
1 shallot, peeled and minced
Salt and freshly ground black pepper to taste
½ cup extra-virgin olive oil
1 large tomato peeled, seeded, and diced

1. Bring a large pot of water to a boil. Drop the asparagus in the water and cook for 3 minutes. Drain the asparagus and immediately plunge it in cold water. Drain well.

2. In a small bowl, whisk together the vinegar, mustard, shallot, salt, and pepper. Slowly drizzle in the olive oil while continuing to whisk.

3. Arrange the asparagus on a serving platter and garnish with the diced tomato. Drizzle on the vinaigrette before serving.

POACHED SALMON FILLETS

1 cup dry white wine
1 onion, coarsely chopped
2 stalks celery, coarsely chopped
1 carrot, coarsely chopped
1 teaspoon peppercorns
1 tablespoon salt
3 bay leaves
6 6-ounce salmon fillets

1. To prepare the court bouillon, bring 2 quarts water to a boil. Add the wine, chopped vegetables, and seasonings, and boil for 20 minutes.

2. Butter a large flame-proof roasting pan and arrange the salmon fillets comfortably in the pan. Strain the court bouillon over the fish. If necessary, place the pan across two burners, and simmer gently for five minutes.

3. Turn off the heat and allow the fish to cool in the liquid to room temperature. Before serving, strain off the liquid. To serve the next day, cover and refrigerate the fish in the liquid. Pour off the liquid before serving with the herb sauce.

HERB SAUCE

½ bunch watercress
2 scallions
1 small bunch dill
½ cup mayonnaise
Salt and freshly ground black pepper to taste

1. Place the watercress, scallions, and dill in the bowl of a food processor, and chop coarsely. Add the mayonnaise and seasonings and process until the herbs are finely chopped.

2. Refrigerate until serving time.

THREE-GRAIN RICE SALAD

2 cups white rice
1 cup Wehani brown rice
½ cup wild rice
8-ounce package frozen artichoke hearts,
*   cooked according to directions and drained*
1 bunch scallions, chopped
6 sun-dried tomatoes, cut into julienne strips
1 cup vegetable oil
½ cup virgin olive oil
½ cup red wine vinegar
1 tablespoon minced garlic
Salt and freshly ground black pepper to taste

1. In separate pots of boiling water cook the white rice for 18 to 20 minutes, the brown rice for 45 minutes, and the wild rice for 1 hour. As each rice finishes cooking, rinse with cold water and drain in a colander. When all three rices are well drained, place them into a mixing bowl, and add the artichoke hearts, scallions, and sun-dried tomatoes.

2. In a bowl, whisk together the remaining ingredients. Pour the dressing over the rice, mix well, and serve.

●

FRUIT TARTS

1½ cups (3 sticks) unsalted butter, cut into
   small pieces
3½ cups all-purpose flour
1 tablespoon sugar
2 large eggs, lightly beaten
1 tablespoon milk
2 cups milk
6 egg yolks
¾ cup sugar
½ teaspoon vanilla
4 tablespoons cornstarch
Strawberries, kiwi, blueberries, whatever is
   fresh and in season
½ cup apricot jam

1. Place the butter, flour, and sugar into the bowl of a food processor. Pulse on and off until the mixture resembles coarse crumbs. Add the eggs and milk and pulse briefly until the dough forms a ball.

2. Remove the dough to a floured board and knead lightly to form a ball. Wrap loosely with plastic wrap and chill for 1 hour.

3. Place the milk in a saucepan over moderate heat and bring to a simmer, stirring constantly with a wooden spoon.

4. In a mixing bowl whisk together the egg yolks, sugar, vanilla, and cornstarch. Slowly pour the milk into the yolk mixture, whisking quickly. Pour the mixture back into the saucepan and place over moderate heat, stirring constantly with a wooden spoon until the mixture thickens. Do not let the mixture boil. Pour the custard back into a bowl, place a piece of plastic wrap directly on top of the custard, and refrigerate until ready to use.

5. Preheat the oven to 350° F. Remove the pastry from the refrigerator and let stand for 10 to 15 minutes, until pliable, before rolling out.

6. On a lightly floured board roll out the pastry. Cut the dough into 6 6-inch circles. Lightly press the dough into 6 4-inch tartlet pans. Line each tartlet pan with a square of foil (shiny side down) and fill with rice or dried beans to prevent the pastry from puffing up during baking, or press on a second mold of the same shape with the bottom buttered.

7. Bake for 15 to 20 minutes. Let the pastry shells cool completely. Before serving, fill each shell with custard. Arrange the fruit decoratively over the custard.

8. To glaze the tarts, melt the apricot jam over low heat and gently brush it onto the fruit.

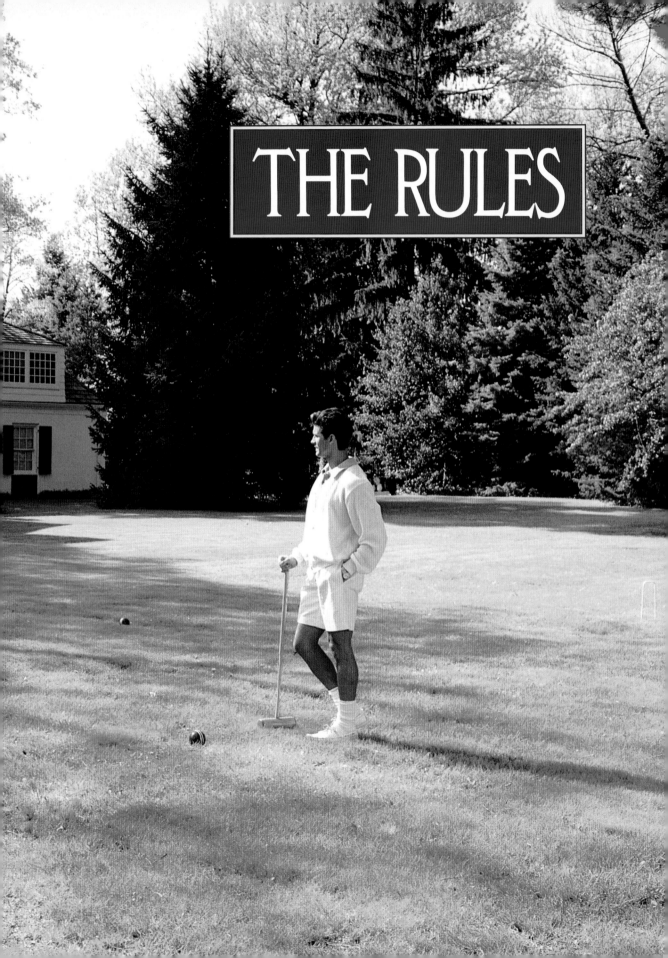

THE RULES

M ore than one hundred years ago, when the game was very fashionable, many companies that manufactured croquet sets also published their own rule books with different sets of rules. Naturally this made for confusion on the courts. When combined with the variations in the equipment, croquet's fall from popularity was understandable.

It seemed impossible to get everyone together on just how the game should be played. Eventually the rules were standardized by a British croquet committee of experts, but American companies chose to ignore their English counterparts and pretty much made things up as they went along.

For example, one fascinating idea from an American rule book of the time concerns the placement of wickets. Three different layouts are offered, and the text suggests that "as the player's knowledge of croquet increases many other positions will suggest themselves." The possible results of encouraging this individual ingenuity boggles the mind and conjures up a picture of wickets placed under bushes or behind trees, making the activity more of an Easter egg hunt than a croquet game. And despite the fact that the idea provided untold opportunities for creativity, such freedom was not conducive to croquet.

Today, strangely enough, it is still possible to find variations in the rules, depending on which manufacturer made your croquet set. But fortunately the regulations have been standardized and updated by the United States Croquet Association, under the leadership of Jack Osborn. Following are the complete United States Croquet Association rules for backyard croquet and golf croquet.

BASIC RULES OF CROQUET
•

USE OF MALLET

1. A player

a. may hold any part of the mallet handle with one or both hands and may use any stance (i.e., center, side, or golf).

b. must hit the ball (not shove or push) with the striking end(s) of the mallet head only once per stroke (no double tap).

2. It shall be counted as a stroke if the mallet hits the wicket or ground but not the ball or misses the ball completely.

3. If a player, in attempting to strike his own ball, touches (with his foot or mallet) another ball, his turn ends and both balls are replaced.

4. The striker may not

a. place another mallet against a ball and then hit it with his own.

b. move or shake a ball by hitting a wicket or stake.

c. touch or strike with his mallet any other ball than his own.

PENALTY for committing a fault under rules 1, 2, 3, and 4: *end of turn,* with replacement of any balls having been moved.

START OF PLAY

5. The toss of a coin (or lots drawn for individual play) determines the choice of order of play. A side may choose to play first or second and shall then play in the order shown on the stake.

6. All balls must start from the starting tee

(from one mallet head to three feet—depending upon court length) behind the first wicket with each side playing alternative turns in the rotation indicated on the stake.

MAKING A WICKET
AND
SCORING POINTS

7. A player's ball passing completely through the first (of first two) wicket(s) scores the wicket point(s) and is entitled to one additional stroke. One stroke (and wicket point) is earned for passing through each succeeding wicket in the order shown in the diagrams on pages 86–89.

8. If a player fails to run wicket number one on his first stroke, his turn ends.

9. A ball stopping in or rolling back into the wicket has not made the wicket nor scored the wicket point.

10. A ball is considered through the wicket when a straight edge placed against the approach side of the wicket does not touch the ball.

11. To score a wicket point, a ball must have *started* to run the wicket from the approach side.

12. A ball which is dead on another ball lying at or in the approach to the wicket may not hit that ball and if it does the wicket is not made, the player's turn ends, and both balls are replaced.

  a. A ball which is dead on another ball laying beyond (not intruding into) the wicket must make complete passage through the wicket, either before or after contact, to score the wicket point and receive one extra stroke.

13. A player may block (stymie) a wicket twice with a ball upon which the opponent is dead, but on the opponent's third turn he must leave the wicket clear or be lifted and replaced after that turn. A ball which is encroaching on the direct path through a wicket is considered to be a block or stymie.

14. In the nine-wicket game a ball hitting the turning stake scores a point, clears any prior deadness, and earns one extra stroke to be played from where it comes to rest. (Not applicable in the six-wicket game.)

  a. A rover ball hitting the finishing stake in its striker's turn (or put against it by another rover) scores the final point for that ball, which is removed from that game.

ROQUET, CROQUET,
AND
EXTRA STROKES

15. During a turn the striker is entitled to hit *(roquet)* each ball (either partner's or opponent's) that he is alive on and thereby earn two additional strokes. The striker's ball then becomes dead on each ball so hit and may not hit it again until he scores his next wicket point for his ball.

  a. In hitting two or more balls upon which it is alive in the same stroke, the roquet will count on the first ball hit with the other being replaced.

  b. A ball which has made a roquet cannot, in that same stroke, score a wicket point.

16. If a striker's ball hits a ball on which it is dead, the striker's turn ends and both balls are replaced.

17. A striker's ball, after making a wicket, which then hits another ball in the same stroke may elect to:

a. hit (roquet) the other ball to earn two strokes or

b. not hit the other ball (and remain alive on it) and take one continuation stroke for having scored the wicket point. (The hit ball is not replaced.)

18. When a roquet is made, the striker's ball becomes a "ball-in-hand" and is brought to where the roqueted ball has come to rest in order to take the first (or *croquet*) stroke of two it has earned.

19. In the croquet stroke the player may either:

a. place his ball in contact with the roqueted ball and in striking it cause both balls to move (or shake) before taking his second shot or:

b. place his ball against the roqueted ball and by holding his ball by foot or hand drive the other away and then play his second shot or:

c. bring his own ball up to a mallet's head away from the roqueted ball and play his two strokes from there.

20. If in the croquet stroke the player plays his shot from a distance greater than a mallet's head from the ball hit *or* if he loses contact with his balls during foot or hand shot, his turn is ended. All balls remain where they lie and no credit is given for wicket or stake points scored in that stroke.

21. If a ball is driven through its wicket by a ball which is alive on it in a roquet stroke or by another ball in its croquet stroke, that ball shall be counted as having scored the wicket point, is cleared of any deadness it may have had, but is not entitled to an extra stroke.

OUT OF BOUNDS

22. A ball is out of bounds when its vertical axis crosses the boundary line (more than halfway over). It shall be replaced on the court one mallet's head from where it first went out or, if near the corner, one mallet's head from the boundary lines.

23. When a player drives his ball through a wicket, so that it comes to rest out of bounds, his turn is ended and the ball shall be placed in bounds one mallet's head from where it went out.

24. At the end of every stroke all balls except the striker's less than a mallet's head from the boundary are placed that length from the line.

a. If the space to which such a ball should be placed be occupied by another ball, the replaced ball shall be put up to a mallet's head in either direction from the said ball (but not touching) at the discretion of the striker.

b. Should two balls be sent over the boundary or less than a mallet's head from the boundary at the same place, the ball first out of bounds or closest to it is placed first with the second placed as in *a.* above.

25. If in a roquet or croquet stroke any ball (except the striker's in the roquet stroke—see rule 26) goes out of bounds, the striker's turn ends and all balls on the court remain where they lie and all balls off the court placed one mallet's head in from the point on the boundary where they went off.

26. If, in making a roquet, the striker's ball goes out of bounds or caroms into a third ball (not the roqueted ball) sending it out, the latter ball is replaced with no penalty and the striker's ball is played as in rule 18.

27. If a ball is roqueted off the court by a striker's ball that is alive on it, the striker's turn ends but he remains alive on the ball so hit.

PLAYING OUT OF TURN
OR
WRONG BALL

28. If a ball is played out of turn, all balls are replaced as at the beginning of play, and the play is resumed in proper sequence with the offending ball losing its next turn in that sequence.

29. If a player plays the wrong ball, his turn ends and all balls are replaced where they were before the fault occurred. In a single's game, a striker playing the wrong partner ball shall be considered to have played out of turn with the penalty as in rule 28.

INTERFERENCE, CALLING
OR
CONDONING FAULTS

30. If a ball is interfered with by an outside agent, except weather or accidentally by an opponent, in any way that materially affects the outcome of the stroke, that stroke shall be replayed. Otherwise, the ball shall be placed, as nearly as can be judged, where it would have come to rest, provided that no point or roquet can thereby be made. A rover ball prevented from scoring the stake by a staked-out ball shall be placed where it would otherwise have come to rest.

31. A fault or misplay by a player should be called as soon as it is discovered but must be called by his opponent before the next turn begins or else it will be automatically condoned.

ROVER AND FINISHING
THE GAME

32. A player who has made all the wickets in the proper sequence becomes rover and is considered alive on all balls.

33. Assuming he is alive on them, a rover ball may hit any other ball only once per turn.

34. After hitting at least two balls, a rover ball may be cleared of deadness by passing through any wicket in any direction (or by hitting the turning stake in the nine-wicket game) and thus earn one continuation stroke.

35. Upon being cleared of deadness on two or three balls, a rover ball may not hit the last ball he was dead on until he hits another ball first whereupon the temporary deadness is also cleared.

36. A rover that runs a wicket in clearing its deadness and in the same stroke hits a ball upon which it was last dead incurs no penalty, and unless either ball is driven out of bounds, both balls remain where they lie and the striker is entitled to take his continuation stroke.

37. A rover's ball can only be driven into the stake by its player or by another rover (either on a roquet or croquet stroke) which is alive on it, whereupon it will be considered to have finished the game (and scored a point for itself), and shall be immediately removed from the court.

38. A rover ball roqueted into the stake by a striker's ball which is dead on it shall be replaced and considered still in play.

39. A rover ball hitting the stake after making roquet is not staked out and shall play normally off the roqueted ball.

40. When one ball of a side (in a team game) has staked out of the game it is removed from the court immediately and play continues in the proper rotation with the staked-out ball losing all subsequent turns.

41. If in a roquet shot a striker's rover ball drives another rover ball into the stake, it is removed from play and the striker receives two strokes taken a mallet's head in any direction from the stake.

42. The game is won by the side (or player) that finishes the game with both balls (or ball) first, or in a time-limit game by the side scoring the highest total of wicket or stake points.

RULES OF GOLF CROQUET

•

Golf croquet is usually played on a six-wicket, one-stake court layout. It may, however, be played on a nine-wicket, two-stake court by modifying the direction of play.

The following rules are based on the six-wicket, one-stake court.

1. The Course

a. Balls are played into the game from one mallet's length from the center stake. In a short version, seven points are contested: the first six and number one again for the seventh point.

b. When thirteen points are contested, the first twelve points are as in croquet. The thirteenth point is the third wicket.

c. When nineteen points are contested, the wickets one back to the rover are contested twice before contesting the third wicket. The stake is not contested.

2. The Game

a. All balls are always for the same wicket in order. The point is scored for the side whose ball first runs the wicket. The game ends as soon as one side has scored a majority of the points to be played (i.e., four out of seven in the short game). It is customary to keep the tally of the score as in match play golf by declaring a side to be one or more points up or down or all square as the case may be.

b. Each turn consists of one stroke. The rules relating to roquet, croquet, and continuation strokes do not apply.

c. The balls are played in the same sequence and color combinations for sides as in basic croquet.

3. Running a Hoop

If a striker causes one of the balls of his side to partly run a wicket during a stroke, such a ball must begin to run such a wicket again before it can be scored by that ball in any subsequent stroke. But if an adversary causes a ball partly to run a wicket during a stroke, it scores both wickets for its side. The wicket point is scored by a ball that is cannoned, peeled or roqueted through a wicket except that a partner ball which has failed to clear a wicket on its own stroke may not be so driven through by his partner unless that ball was put into the wicket by an opponent.

4. Jump Shot

A player may not deliberately make his ball rise from the ground. If he does so accidentally, or in ignorance of this law, and in consequence runs a wicket for his striker's or partner's ball, the point shall not be scored. Likewise, if as a consequence thereof any balls are displaced, such balls may be replaced at the option of the adversary side.

5. Advancing a Ball Prematurely for the Next Point

A player must play so as to contest the wicket in its proper order rather than seek to gain an advantage for the next wicket in order. But a player contesting the wicket in order by, for example, attempting to cannon another ball, may legitimately play the stroke at the strength calculated to bring his ball to rest nearer the next wicket in order.

6. Playing Out of Turn or with a Wrong Ball

If the striker plays out of turn or with the wrong ball, that stroke and any subsequent strokes are null and void. All balls shall be replaced: The right ball shall be played by the correct player, and the other balls shall follow in due sequence. No points made during the period of error shall be scored.

CROQUET COURTS

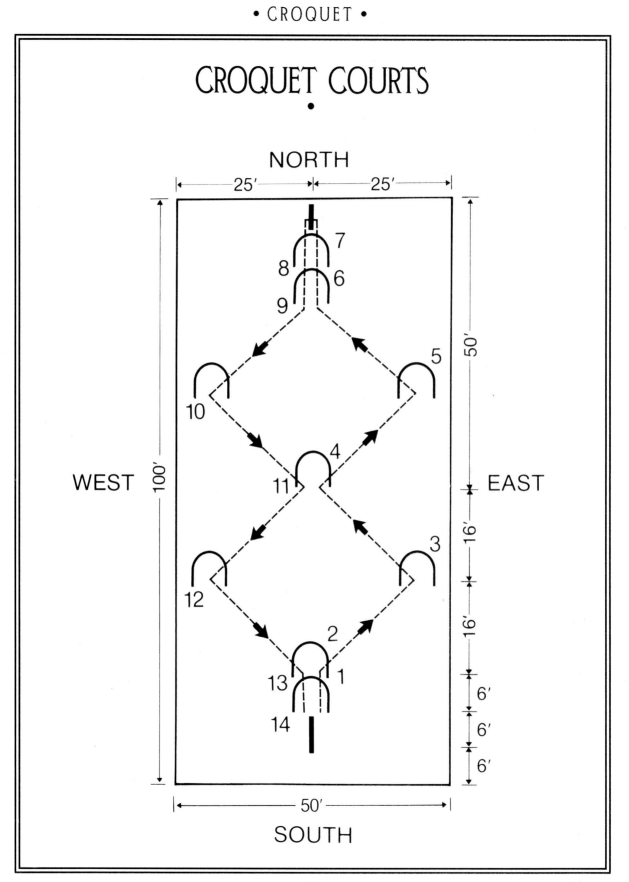

As long as the proportions remain approximately the same (the length should be twice the width), croquet courts can be virtually any size. The diagrams on pages 86 through 88 detail court sizes for backyard play.

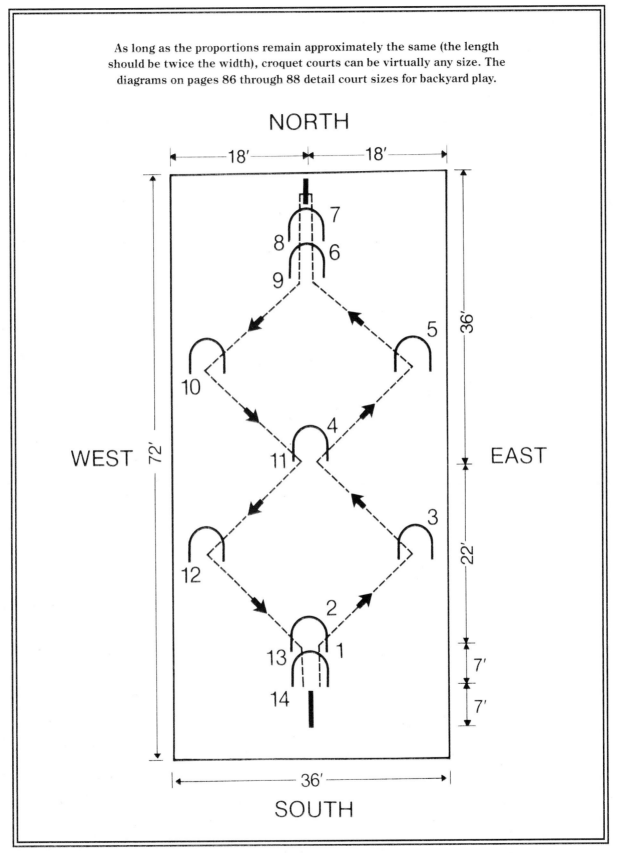

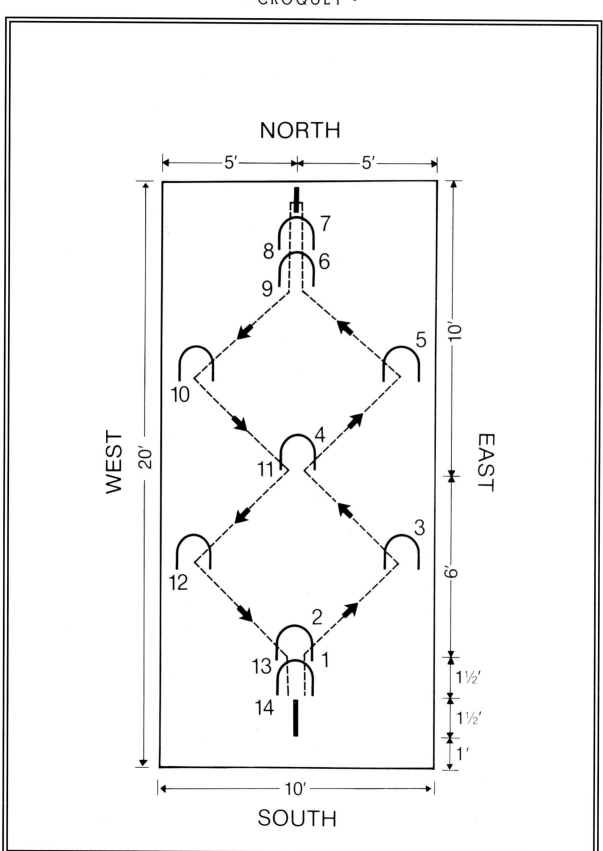

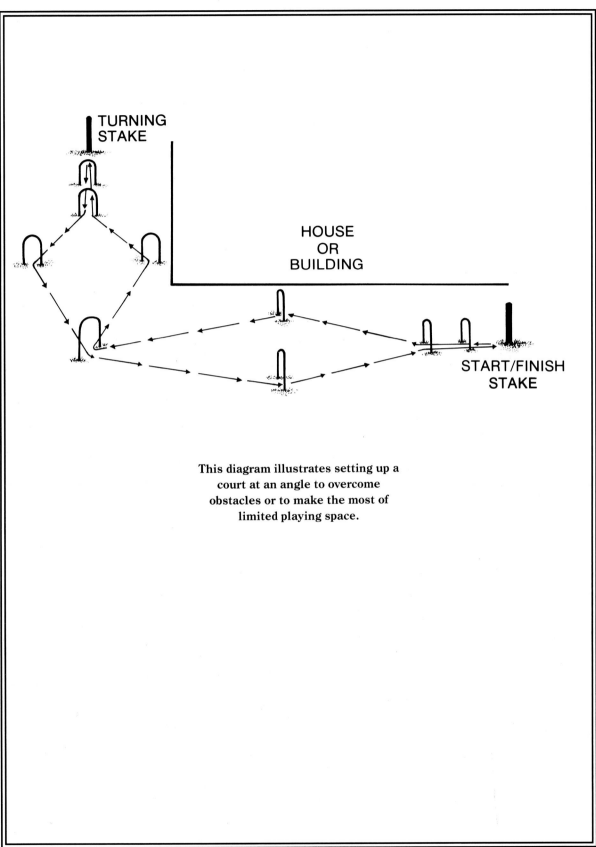

TURNING
STAKE

HOUSE
OR
BUILDING

START/FINISH
STAKE

This diagram illustrates setting up a
court at an angle to overcome
obstacles or to make the most of
limited playing space.

SOURCE GUIDE

For information on where to purchase the fashions and croquet sets that appear in this book, write or call the companies listed below for the nearest retail outlet.

FASHIONS

•

Carole Amper, Inc.
26 W. Seventeenth Street
New York, NY 10011
Children's hats

Crystal Creations
from D & E Accessories
389 Fifth Avenue
New York, NY 10016
Hosiery

Ellen Tracy
Women's sportswear; available at better department stores

Eric Javits
Hats; available at better department stores

James River Traders
James River Landing
Hampton, VA 23631
1-800-445-2405
Men's and women's sportswear; write or call for mail-order catalogue

Jessica McLintock
Women's sportswear; available at better department stores

Land's End
Land's End Lane
Dodgeville, WI 53595
1-800-356-4444
Men's and women's sportswear; write or call for mail-order catalogue

Le Coq Sportif
1-800-524-2377
Activewear and sportswear

L.L. Bean
Freeport, ME 04033
1-800-221-4221
Men's and women's sportswear; write or call for mail-order catalogue

Makins
Hats; available at better department stores

Nancy Crystal
Women's sportswear; available at better department stores

Pasargada
902 Madison Avenue
New York, NY 10021
Sportswear

Randy Kemper, Inc.
Women's sportswear; available at better department stores

Robert Stock
Men's sportswear; available at better department stores

Schatzle
1-800-268-8276
Girl's Dresses

Suri de Khan
Boy's clothing; available at children's boutiques and specialty stores

Forster Manufacturing Co., Inc.
P.O. Box 756
Wilton, ME 04294
1-800-341-7574
Available at sporting goods and specialty stores

General Sportcraft Co., Inc.
140 Woodbine Street
Bergenfield, NJ 07621
Available at sporting goods and specialty stores

Hammacher Schlemmer
(Forster for Hammacher Schlemmer)
147 E. Fifty-seventh Street
New York, NY 10022
1-800-543-3366
Available at their stores and through mail-order catalogue

Jaques of London
Croquet International
635 Madison Avenue
New York, NY 10022
212-688-5495

Spalding
Available at sporting goods and toy stores

CROQUET SETS
•

Abercrombie & Fitch
1-800-231-9715
Available from their stores and through mail-order catalogue

Fisher-Price
1-800-828-7315
Children's set; available at toy stores

If you are interested in information about the competitive sport of croquet, contact:
The United States Croquet Association
500 Avenue of Champions
Palm Beach Gardens, FL 33418
1-305-627-3999

CREDITS

STAFF

Game's master, Lawrence J. Gazlay; stylist, Gabriela Hirsh; hair and makeup, Michael D'Apice, Vinnie Ferrara, Kathleen Murphy, Glen Solberg; catering coordinator, Christine Cavanagh, The Event Group, New York City; food, Steve Heinzerling, Heinzerling Caterers, Brooklyn, New York; food stylist, Michael Ereshena, S. Michael, Park Slope, New York; illustrations, Ray Aronne, New Dawn Productions; asst. stylist, Jody B. Ross; photographer's asst., Paul Schouten.

Models: David Bell, Crystal Bennett, Maggi Benninger, Jerry Bilden, Helen Parrish Brown, Kate Bruggeman, Peter J. Campbell, Enda Carroll, Robert Collins, Blake Daniels, Ali Espley, Edmund L. Flory, Lawrence J. Gazlay, Cathy Haala, Karen Ann Huner, Nicholas Kitsopoulas, Steven Meek, Cheryl Morgan, Fanny Olyphant, Pamela Olyphant, Dean Ostrum, Kristy Pallas, Rhonda Lynn Pecoraro, Michael Ragan, Jeffrey M. Snyder, Craig Uher, Susan Van Horn, Richard O. Villella, Marcie Wyrick, Tom Young, and Kris.

Modeling Agencies: Big Beauties, DEA Model Agency, Ferarri Models, Ford Men, L'Image Models, Powers Models, Slique, Van Der Veer Models, West Models, Wilhelmina Men.

CROQUET EQUIPMENT

Abercrombie and Fitch, Fisher Price (children's set), Forster, Forster for Hammacher Schlemmer, John Jaques, Spaulding, General Sportcraft.

FASHIONS

Men's Sportswear: Land's End, L.L. Bean, James River Traders, Robert Stock, Le Coq Sportif.

Women's Sportswear: Scott McLintock, Eric Javits, Ellen Tracy, L.L. Bean, James River Traders, Randolph Kemper, Land's End, Makins, Pasargada, hosiery by Crystal Creations Apparel Inc., Hats by Makins Hats.

Children's Fashions: Schatzle, Carol Amper, Suri de Khan.

LOCATIONS

Location coordinator, Rosemary Haness, Chairperson, New Jersey Historical Society, Plainfield.

Homes: Courtesy Paul and Michele Rawson; Drake House, Tom Ricketts, Ed Santiago; Longfellow House, Mr. Wigten; Webster House, Mr. and Mrs. Sutton; Dr. George Lane; Monday Afternoon Club, the organization; Dr. Barylick.

ACKNOWLEDGMENTS

The author is especially grateful to the many individuals and organizations who acted as resources for valuable and vital information, particularly Jack Osborn, President, United States Croquet Association, and Jesse Kornbluth, whose insights and instructions first appeared in *Winning Croquet,* published by Simon and Schuster. Also, the Milton Bradley Company, Abercrombie and Fitch, General Sportcraft, Forster, Hammacher Schlemmer, and the staffs of the New York Public Library Research Department and the East Hampton Free Library were particularly helpful.

Particular thanks are also due my agent, Harvey Klinger, who suggested I do this book, and to RoseAnne Vecchione and Frank Hodgkins.

It is impossible to properly express adequate appreciation to the remarkable staff of talented and creative individuals who invested long hours in making sure that everything was right. Special gratitude is owed to Executive Editor Harriet Bell and Design Director Ken Sansone, whose confidence and enthusiasm were a joy to experience, and to the backbone crew of Gabriela Hirsh, Michael D'Apice, and Lawrence Gazlay, who were remarkable. Also, unquestionably, the talent and vision of John Falocco is evidenced by his photographs, which bring this book to life.

INDEX